THE
Finnegans Wake
EXPERIENCE

also by Roland McHugh

THE SIGLA OF FINNEGANS WAKE
Edward Arnold, London
University of Texas Press, Austin

'the most authoritative and enlightening exegesis of *Finnegans Wake* that has yet appeared' J.S. Atherton, *British Book News*.

'McHugh has written the best criticism of *Finnegans Wake* anywhere in *The Sigla of Finnegans Wake*' Anthony Farrow, *Cithara*.

'Roland McHugh's book is by far the best account of *Finnegans Wake* (*FW*) for over a decade. It is a model of clarity and scholarship and repeats only the most meaningful results of earlier research. Thus anyone approaching *FW* for the first time could not find a better guide, and indeed most previous texts now appear out-dated' Ian MacArthur, *Irish University Review*.

'Can there be a book about *FW* which one would recommend both to neophytes and to experienced Wakers staggering under the burden of the growing mass of explications? I wouldn't have thought it possible, but *The Sigla of Finnegans Wake* comes as near as never mind to being that book. For the veteran Waker, it avoids almost entirely repeating explanations already known, and provides instead a large amount of interesting and hitherto unpublished information relevant to particular identifications and allusions. For the beginning reader, it provides a guide to the structural relationships of the book, and an overview of the 'narrative' in terms of this structure . . . I am convinced that the sigla approach is as much of a breakthrough in FW studies as one could hope for at this stage' Louis O. Mink, *A Wake Newslitter*.

'McHugh's firm and careful presentation of the distinct tone and balance of each section of *FW* is of far greater value in appreciating Joyce's last book than is any simplified

or predigested shortened *FW*' Mark L. Troy, *Irish Studies Newsletter*.

'Roland McHugh in his exemplary study of the *Sigla* is innovative in a more fruitful way: he knows as much as anyone of what Joyce knew, but he examines Joyce in the creative act, and instead of inert knowledge provides an Ariadne's clew indespensable to all future adventurers into the daedalian labyrinth . . . it is the only exegetical work I know of that forces the reader back into *FW* instead of obviating the necessity to read it, and offering a consolation prize instead, and therefore becomes the only safe exegetical work to use in teaching *FW*' Brendan O Hehir, *Novel — A Forum on Fiction*. 'Reading Mr McHugh's book has been for me a quick refresher course in the *Wake*; I hope it appears in paperback in time for my next *Wake* seminar. Instead of paraphrasing Joyce, as most handbooks do, it presses the student to read for himself and keeps constantly before him the ideal of seeing *Finnegans Wake* as a coherent whole' Vivian Mercier, *TLS*.

'His extensive knowledge of the text, his care in relating every detail to the over-arching structure, and his objective devotion to the pure text itself carry one deeply into Joyce's masterpiece' Robert Boyle, SJ, *Modern Fiction Studies*.

and

ANNOTATIONS TO FINNEGANS WAKE
Johns Hopkins University Press, Baltimore
Routledge, Kegan Paul, London

Roland McHugh

THE
Finnegans Wake
EXPERIENCE

IRISH ACADEMIC PRESS
Dublin

This book was typeset in the Republic of Ireland and printed in Great Britain for Irish Academic Press Ltd., Kill Lane, Kill-o'-the Grange, Blackrock, County Dublin, Ireland.

Cased edition ISBN 0 7165 0047 7
Limp edition ISBN 0 7165 0065 5

ACKNOWLEDGEMENTS

For extracts from *Finnegans Wake* I should like to thank the Society of Authors as the literary representative of the Estate of James Joyce, and the Viking Press (Viking Penguin Inc.). Material from the Buffalo notebooks is © the Trustees of the James Joyce Estate 1981, and quoted by permission of the Poetry/Rare Books Collection, University Libraries, State University of New York at Buffalo. A quotation from R.M. Adams' *Surface and Symbol* is included by permission of the Oxford University Press.

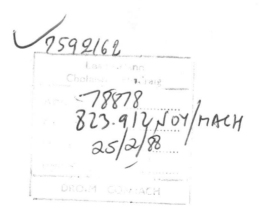

Contents

1
Samples

James Joyce is a fashionable writer and his last book, *Finnegans Wake*, is frequently named in awe and reverence by all kinds of literati. There is a great deal of bluff in this naming, for few prospective readers actually sustain their curiosity for more than a page or two. If they want to know more, they usually turn to guidebooks and commentaries, substituting printed doctrines for direct confrontation with Joyce's text. *Finnegans Wake* is seen distantly and from without, like a darkened powerhouse on the skyline.

I suppose I have a natural distrust of gurus. I spent almost three years reading *Finnegans Wake* (abbreviated FW) before looking at any kind of critical account. I contrived to retain this innocence until I had formulated a coherent system of interpretation. I was then able to evaluate the guidebooks from a neutral vantage point and elude indoctrination. Of course, I learned valuable things from them, and had often to discard illformed conclusions in consequence. But this seemed a healthy process, although its duration grotesquely exceeded the time any reasonable person would devote to a book. I hardly intend that my present readers should repeat my example, but I feel that the experience qualifies me to introduce FW to them in a particularly helpful manner.

Before I describe the stages in a solitary exposure to FW it will be as well to look at a few specimens of the opus. As FW is divided into four Books, each having its distinct atmosphere, we will discuss an excerpt from each Book. The excerpts will be reasonably representative of their Books, and our discussion will illustrate generalities important in many other parts of the *Wake*.

The first extract, from Book I, runs from line 1 to line 15 on page 162 (any edition), and is conventionally labelled 162.01-15:

> The older sisars (Tyrants, regicide is too good for you!) become unbeurrable from age, (the compositor of the farce of dustiny however makes a thunpledrum mistake by letting off this pienofarte effect as his furst act as that is where the juke comes in) having been sort-of-nineknived and chewly removed (this soldier - author - batman for all his commontoryism is just another of those souftsiezed bubbles who never quite got the sandhurst out of his eyes so that the champaign he draws for us is as flop as a plankrieg) the twinfreer types are billed to make their reupprearance as the knew kneck and knife knickknots on the deserted *champ de bouteilles.* (A most cursery reading into the Persic-Uraliens hostery shows us how Fonnumagula picked up that propper numen out of a colluction of prifixes though to the permienting cannasure the Coucousien oafsprung of this sun of a kuk is as sattin as there's a tub in Tobolosk)

A good deal of Book I has this tone—a commentary on some story or letter. Most of the material in parentheses forms a sort of reconsidered secondary comment on its author and origins. If we ignore this, it should not be too hard to see that the story concerns the assassination of Caesar. The older Caesars become unbearable from age. Having been knifed to death and duly removed, the twin brothers (French, *frères*)—and freers (for they endeavour to free Caesar's people from his tyranny)—are, according to the playbill, to make their reappearance, uprearing, as the new neck-and-neck knick-knacks on the deserted *champ de bateilles.*

Should the reader at this point glance through the region of FW between pages 161 and 168 he will find the Julius Caesar plot everywhere. Brutus and Cassius, disguised as butter (Burrus) and cheese (Caseous), occur frequently as twin brothers. Take 161.15-19: 'Burrus, let us like to imagine, is a genuine prime, the real choice, full of natural greace, the mildest of milkstoffs yet unbeaten as a risicide and, of course, obsoletely unadulterous whereat Caseous is obversely the revise of him and in fact not an ideal choose by any meals'. Therefore 'unbeurrable from age' can be seen to contain French *beurre* and *fromage,* butter and cheese. And we can quote Brendan O Hehir's gloss on 'regicide is too good for you': 'among the motives for assassinating Caesar was his apparent desire to become king (*rex*); he was already *tyrannos,* so his murder was *tyrannicide* to forestall the necessity for it to be *regicide*'.[1]

Other stories are clearly comprehended besides Caesar's. The 'farce of dustiny'—and admittedly everyone's eventual destiny is, like Caesar's, to become dust—echoes Verdi's opera *La Forza del*

Destino, but is distinguished by its composer's mistake: his first act is to let off a musically unsound triple trumpet kettledrum effect on the pianoforte, a thunder-drum sound like a full (Italian, *pieno*) fart. Now, if we look at the opening page of FW, just such an effect appears in lines 15-17: 'The fall (bababadal-gharaghtakamminarronnkonnbronntonnerronntuonn-thunntrovarrhounawnskawntoohoohoordenenthurnu-k!)'. This is made out of various foreign equivalents of 'thunder', for instance Japanese *kaminari,* Italian *tuono,* Portugese *trovāo* and Danish *tordenen.*[2] Its significance has generally been agreed upon since Samuel Beckett's authorised essay on the *Wake* appeared in 1929. It represents the roll of thunder which, according to Giambattista Vico's *The New Science*, characterises the first phase through which all human civilisations must progress. Vico was an astonishingly original thinker of the early eighteenth century, and Joyce, who admired him, stated unambiguously that FW was an expression of Vico's philosophy. Beckett's essay attempts 'to condense the thesis of Vico, the scientific historian. In the beginning was the thunder: the thunder set free Religion, in its most objective and unphilosophical form—idolatrous animism: Religion produced Society, and the first social men were the cave-dwellers, taking refuge from a passionate Nature: this primitive family life receives its first impulse towards development from the arrival of terrified vagabonds: admitted, they are the first slaves: growing stronger, they exact agrarian concessions, and a despotism has evolved into a primitive feudalism: the cave becomes a city, and the feudal system a democracy: then an anarchy: this is corrected by a return to monarchy: the last stage is a tendency towards interdestruction: the nations are dispersed, and the Phoenix of Society arises out of their ashes.' [3] Caesar's assassination occupies a conspicuous step in the cycle, much of Vico's data deriving from his studies in Roman history.

The 'farce of dustiny' then, is partly FW itself, with the 'pienofarte effect' in its first act. That's where the joke comes in. The 'juke', who also comes in, as the 'furst' (German *Furst,* prince), is that 'good Dook Umphrey' whose exploits feature at another early stage in the *Wake*, occupying most of its second chapter.

The next parenthesised clause delineates the 'compositor'. He is soldier and batman as well as author, and we may regard his account of Caesar's fall as a specimen of military history. But for all his commentaries, and for all his political persuasions (it is quite immaterial whether these are 'common toryism' or communism) he is, for the narrator of this portion of FW, a mere 'South Sea Bubble'. This was a short-lived scheme of 1720 to take up the British National Debt by trade with the South Seas. The compositor, then, is an ephemeral wonder. He has never properly woken up ('got the sand out of his eyes'). His strategy was learned at Sandhurst Military Academy rather than directly in the wars, so the campaign he sketches for us is lifeless—as flat as a pancake, a flop as colourless as a plan of the war (German, *Krieg*[4]) . He does not stimulate our senses, merely provides glasses of flat (i.e. non-effervescent) champagne.

Brutus and Cassius, the rivals, running neck-and-neck, are billed (and built) to reappear on the battle-field, which is also a bottlefield (French, *champ de bouteilles*). It is this italicized phrase to which the next sentence refers, though that might not be immediately apparent to you. One of the commonest difficulties encountered in FW is that of seeing the thread which connects adjacent sentences. If we ignore the qualification ('though . . .Tobolosk') we see it stated that a most cursory (and cursing) reading of this history shows us how the compositor, now called 'Fonnumagula', picked up that proper name (Latin, *nomen*[1]) '*champ de bouteilles*' out of a collection of prefaces or prefixes. But, says the quali-fication, to the permitting connoisseur, the Caucasian origin (spring) of the phrase is as certain as there's a tail on a cat. And its offspring, i.e. the phrases deri-ving from it, are Caucasian.

The longest military parody in FW is Buckley's shooting of the Russian General during the Crimean War (FW 338-355), hence the notion that a *Wake* battlefield should ultimately lie in Russia, in the Caucasus.[5] Tobol'sk is a town in Siberia[5], and in 'Persic-Uraliens' one notices the Urals[5] along with some Persian aliens. But Napoleon's campaigns are also pertinent (as at FW 008-010), hence the in-clusion of the phrase 'Corsican upstart'. Here we may mark a further sub-narrative. We ought to be discus-sing a 'proper name' found in a collection of prefaces, but '*champ de bouteilles*' is not a proper name. The acquisition of a proper name is really another theme from the second chapter of FW, which explains the origin of Duke Humphrey's surname 'Earwicker'. 'Persic-Uraliens' echoes a phrase in that chapter (038. 11: 'no persicks and armelians;') but more dramatically it echoes *Persse O'Reilly,* the name given to Earwicker in the ballad closing the chapter. The ballad is composed by somebody called Hosty, hence 'Persic-Uraliens hostery'.

By now you are probably finding the personages emerging from the text a problem. Let me presume to simplify things: everyone so far named, except Brutus, Cassius and Hosty, is an aspect of a single composite personality. In his manuscripts Joyce represents Caesar, Earwicker, Persse O'Reilly (French, *perce-oreille,* earwig), Finnegan, Finn MacCool and many others, by a sign (technically, a *siglum*),ᴍ.

Tim Finnegan, hero of the Irish-American ballad 'Finnegan's Wake', is a builder who falls from his ladder and is assumed dead, but resurrects at his wake. In the first chapter of FW he is conflated with the legendary Irish giant, Finn MacCool, for example at 006.13-15, immediately after the fall: 'Macool, Macool, orra whyi deed ye diie? of a trying thirstay mournin? Sobs they sighdid at Fillagain's chrissormiss wake'. Finn MacCool is clearly the principal echo in the name of our compositor - author - soldier - batman, 'Fonnumagula'. We have been told that Finn MacCool picked up a proper name in the Persse O'Reillyan history. In other words, when ᴍ advanced from the first to the second FW chapter he obtained a significant new name, which in fact helped to prop up his precarious reputation, and was thus a 'propper numen'.

Before leaving the passage we may note a few sub-
sidiary components. Despite the appearance of
Finnish words lower on 162, *sisar,* meaning sister, is
probably irrelevant as the tyrant is quite unequivo-
cally male. Perhaps he is a 'sizar'. In *Ulysses,* the
fatherly George Russell (AE) is said to have 'a sizar's
laugh of Trinity', but his use in FW is rather periph-
eral. ⋔ is built from numerous avatars, some of
whom fall for good, but most somehow resurrect. So
Caesar is 'sort-of-nineknived': he is like a cat of nine
lives. He is 'chewly removed' by his butter and cheese
assassins. Some versions of the death of ⋔ elsewhere
in FW involve ritual cannibalism in parody of Frazer's
The Golden Bough, and this helps to justify the
eating overtone.

Perhaps French *souffler,* to blow, can be discerned
within 'souftsiezed'—the bubble has, after all, to be
blown. It's harder to account for the alliteration in
'knew kneck and knife knickknots', though 561.02
does equate the twins with a fork and knife. Obviously some component in 'Fonnumagula' remains un-
identified, but *numen* is Latin for divine will[1], so the
new name acquired by Humphrey apparently confers
some sort of divine authority. This must necessarily
proceed from God, that 'collector of prepuces'[6], but
also from a contest (Latin, *colluctatio*[1]) of prefixes.
In fact several other potential names for Humphrey
are suggested in the second chapter of FW: 'a turn-
piker who is by turns a pikebailer no seldomer than
an earwigger!' ⋔ is in one sense a sun-god but in the
military context he is a 'son of a gun', and in the eating context the son of a cook (in 'kuk'). Possibly

Swift's *Tale of a Tub*, occasionally mentioned in FW, contributes to the 'tub in Tobolosk', which has been sat in, but though I can envisage further glosses on 'permienting cannasure' I have little faith in them. In fact, in the three remaining excerpts I shall ignore glosses which do not contribute meaningfully to the demonstrable context, so in all cases my explanation will be somewhat incomplete.

FW must always mean many things at once. In the piece just considered there is a battlefield which is also a bottlefield—a table with food and bottles on it. Is the 'compositor' trying to explain some point of strategy by moving the butter, cheese, etc. about to represent parties in conflict? Only on one level. Unfortunately, the balancing act of keeping one's attention fluid between all the levels defeats most readers, who trust one level and pay lip-service to the others. Perhaps a more extreme example will show the fallacy in that approach.

Joyce is reported to have said 'Time and the river and the mountain are the real heroes of my book'.[7] It's well known that in FW the concepts of the human female and the river are somehow conflated, although how one takes that appears to be a matter of taste. One many exalt woman by comparison with the majesty of clear flowing water, or one may degrade her by depicting the rivermouth as a gargantuan urinogenital orifice. But Joyce treats both attitudes as cliché and instead spotlights fortuitous parallelism with a consequent split image and throwaway humour. In our Book II excerpt (327.09-23) the tailor's daughter is described to the Norwegian

Captain in such a way that we are continually obliged to construe her in both human and aquatic terms:

> with a grit as hard as the trent of the thimes but a touch as saft as the dee in flooing and never a Hyderow Jenny the like of her lightness at look and you leap, rheadoromanscing long evmans invairn, about little Anny Roners and all the Lavinias of ester yours and pleding for them to herself in the periglus glatsch hangs over her trickle bed, it's a piz of fortune if it never falls from the stuffel, and, when that mallaura's over till next time and all the prim rossies are out dressparading and the tubas tout tout for the glowru of their god, making every Dinny dingle after her down the Dargul dale and (wait awhile, blusterbuss, you're marchadant too forte and don't start furlan your ladins till you've learned the lie of her landuage!), when it's summwer calding and she can hear the pianutunar beyant the bayondes in Combria sleepytalking to the Wiltsh muntons, titting out through her droemer window for the flyend of a touchman over the wishtas of English Strand

Book II is definitely more complicated than any of the other three and this extract possesses a difficulty whose justification does not concern us right now. To understand what is being said you will need to identify a number of words belonging to an ancient language called Rhaeto-Romanic, or Roumansch, which is spoken in certain Swiss cantons. Also, as a Norwegian is being addressed, there are Norwegian words present. Fortunately, lists of the Rhaeto-Romanic[8] and Norwegian[9] elements in FW can be obtained, and with their assistance we can proceed.

On the aquatic plane, the grit of the river-bed is as hard as that found in the river Trent and the river

Thames, but the touch of its water is as soft (Norwegian, *saft*, juice) as that of the river Dee in flooding. On the human plane, the anger (Rhaeto-Romanic, *gritta*) of the daughter is as hard as the trend of the times demands, yet she has a touch as imperceptible as the letter *d* which has been removed in the word 'flooing'. Both the water and the girl are very light, and they are, therefore, compared with hydrogen, the lightest element, impetuously failing to look before they leap. 'Look and you leap' sounds like a children's game, at which the girl presumably excels.

The Rhaeto-Romanic (RR) *inviern* means winter, and the first part of our passage considers the situation in winter. The girl reads romances all the long evenings in vain: they may be written in Rhaeto-Romanic but they concern persons such as 'Little Annie Rooney', the subject of a popular song[10], and heroines with names like Lavinia and Ester. Swift's friends Esther Johnson (Stella) and Esther Vanhomrigh (Vanessa), who frequently manifest conjointly in FW, may be detected.[11] But the river's preferred reading encompasses geophysical enormities. 'Anny... Lavinias' reflects the name Anna Liffey, given on old maps of Dublin's principal river, and *lavina* is RR for an avalanche. The river is inspired by thoughts of great waterways and the avalanches of yesteryear, and foreign places (RR *ester*, foreign) towards which it might flow.

Both the girl and the river have a bed. The girl is pleading (RR *pled*, a word) for the heroines as she looks into the pierglass hanging over her truckle bed (a low bed on castors). The stream, undoubtedly young and narrow, looks into the dangerous (RR *prigulus*; Welsh *peryglus*) ice (RR *glatsch*) overhanging its bed. It's a piece of fortune if the mirror never falls from the ladder-rung (German, *Stufe*)[12] supporting it, and a peak (RR *piz*) of fortune if the wind (RR *suffel*) doesn't blow down the ice.

So much for the winter. When that bad weather (RR *malaura*) is over until next year and all the primroses come up on the riverbanks, the rossies (Dublin slang for an impudent girl, a 'forward piece') are out parading their spring dresses. The parade boasts tubas tooting for the glory of God, and also (from the non-human platform) the glory of the forest (RR *god*). Both girl and river look attractive in a spring setting, and every Dinny (Irish *duine,* person)[13] feels a tingle as he watches them pass. The river is here the Dargle, tumbling from the Wicklow Mountains; RR *dargun* is a mountain torrent.

The parenthetical admonition warns the girl's admirer that he is marching too loudly (Italian, *forte*) or too quickly (Norwegian, *fort*), with acknowledgements to Margadant, who wrote a study of Rhaeto-Romanic.[8] Courtship by blustering busses (archaic: kisses) is unlikely to succeed. Don't start following the leaders/ladies until you've learned the lie of the land. Don't start furling a flag inscribed in the Ladin dialect of RR until you've learned that language. (Also RR *furlan* means a little rascal.)

The verb 'titting' is qualified by the two clauses beginning 'when that mallaura's over' and 'when it's summwer calding'. When summer's calling, or it's somewhere hot (Italian, *caldo*) the girl can hear a piano-tuner in a nearby room (RR *combra*) trying to get to sleep by counting sheep (French, *moutons*). I suppose he might be the (sexually uninteresting) blind piano-tuner of *Ulysses*, although RR *tunêr* (to thunder) evokes the voice of **m**. For the river, he is beyond the beyonds, beyond the waves (Italian, *onde*) of Dublin Bay, in Wales (Cambria), talking to the Welsh Mountains (RR *munt*). The pairing of male mountain and female river is a commonplace in FW, so it is reasonable that the river should yearn for the Welsh Mountains (visible from the Wicklow ones on especially clear days). The girl, however, peeps (Norwegian, *titte*) out of her dormer window, dreaming (Norwegian, *drömmer,* dreams) of her future lover.

This entire speech is part of that made to the Norwegian Captain to encourage his courtship of the tailor's daughter, and he has previously been described by the tailor as a 'bugganeering wanderducken' (323.01). Van der Decken is the captain of the *Flying Dutchman*, so the girl is represented as wishing 'for the flyend of a touchman'. Mention lower on 327 of Kilbarrack, Dollymount and the Blue Lagoon suggest that she is in one of the houses on the Clontarf Road, in North-East Dublin, many of which have dormer windows facing across the strand of Bull Island towards the English and Welsh coasts. The river Dargle, by contrast, is on the South side of Dublin, so there is a transpicuous geographical separation of human and natural modes of interpretation.

Obviously, your appreciation of this kind of thing depends upon your sense of humour. For many people, something intended to make you laugh, whatever else it may do, is intrinsically worthless: a joke is not information. Weirdness fails to appeal to them. FW, however, contrives to be simultaneously ridiculous and sublime, whilst casually reconciling many other apparent contraries. One progresses along its path and unveils wonders, but if one is consciously questing for the secret of the universe failure is inevitable. Our Book III excerpt (478.08-22) intimates as much:

> I am told by our interpreter, Hanner Esellus, that there are fully six hundred and six ragwords in your malherbal Magis landeguage in which wald wand rimes alpman and there is resin in all roots for monarch but yav hace not one pronouncable teerm that blows in all the vallums of tartallaght to signify majestate, even provisionally, nor no rheda rhoda or torpentine path or hallucinian via nor aurellian gape nor sunkin rut nor grossgrown trek nor crimeslaved cruxway and no moorhens cry or mooner's plankgang there to lead us to hopenhaven. Is such the *unde derivatur* casematter messio! Frankly. *Magis megis enerretur mynus hoc intelligow.*
>   —How? C'est mal prononsable, tartagliano, perfrances. Vous n'avez pas d'o dans votre boche provenciale, mousoo. Je m'incline mais *Moy jay trouvay la clee dang les champs.* Hay sham nap poddy velour, come on!

The first of these two speeches is delivered by one of a group of four old men seeking to discover ꍈ in name and person. The reply is made by a composite character called 'Yawn', who includes two separate persons prominent elsewhere in FW. One of these is St Patrick, and Yawn's speech uses a great deal of French on account of Patrick's French origins. The other is a child named Kevin, who in 110.22-111.33 observes a hen digging a valuable letter out of an ancient burial-heap.

As elsewhere in Book III, the old men employ as their interpreter an ass (German, *Esel*[14]; Latin, *asellus*[15]). The ass has told them that in the Magi's language used by Yawn there are six hundred and six words, and of them one word (German, *Wort*) rimes, i.e. celebrates, 'alpman', a man as tall as the Alps. Also, he says, in all the roots of these words there is reason for, reason to suppose, 'monarch' implicit. But the language has not one pronounceable term in all its volumes to signify ᛗ, a monarch as tall as the Alps, or as big as a state, 'majestate'. 'All the volumes of Tallaght' suggests the celebrated and lengthy *Martyrology of Tallaght,* compiled at the monastery there.

At the same time that he seeks a name for ᛗ the questioner desires a manifest sign of ᛗ. To understand why this is a plant we must sympathise with Yawn/Patrick's standpoint. God is not a man as big as a state: He is the Trinity, and the signature of the Trinity may be read upon the shamrock. From the botanical plane there are 606 ragworts (pronounced 'ragwerts') in Yawn's bad herbal, the wood (German, *Wald*[14]) contains meaningful wands (sticks), and all the roots of the monarch-like trees contain resin. But Yawn also subsumes the personality of the finder of treasure in burial mounds, Kevin. As such he has directed the seekers to the vallums (earthworks, i.e. mounds) of Tallaght. P.W.Joyce's account of the locale explains why:

> The first leader of a colony after the flood was Parth-
> alon, who, with his followers, ultimately took up his
> residence on the plain anciently called *Sean-mhagh-*
> *Ealta-Edair* [Shan-va-alta-edar], the old plain of the
> flocks of Edar, which stretched along the coast by
> Dublin, from Tallaght to *Edar,* or Howth. The legend—
> which is given in several very ancient authorities—relates
> that after the people of this colony had lived there for
> 300 years, they were destroyed by a plague, which in
> one week carried off 5,000 men and 4,000 women; and
> they were buried in a place called, from this circum-
> stance, *Taimhleacht-Mhuintire-Parthaloin* (Four Mast.),
> the *Tavlaght* or plague-grave of Parthalon's people. This
> place, which lies about five miles from Dublin, still
> retains the name *Taimhleacht,* modernized to Tallaght;
> and on the hill, lying beyond the village, there is to be
> seen at this day a remarkable collection of ancient
> sepulchral tumuli, in which cinerary urns are found in
> great numbers.[16]

Despite their perusal of all this vale of tears the old
men have found not one pronounceable tear signify-
ing ⋔. Nor any path thence towards him. There is
an impressive list of paths, nine of them, that the old
men have failed to discover. Besides looking like 'red
road', 'rheda rhoda' suggests to Louis Mink the
Rhaetian road, 'the main ancient road crossing the
Alps in Swiss territory'.[17] The 'Torpentine path'
could be 'Tarquintine', i.e. the funeral path between
Tarquinia, the chief city of the Etruscans, and its
famous necropolis. There is a botanical allusion again,
to turpentine trees, and a suggestion of torpor. That
is, the path may be a mystical one, to be encountered
in a trance, as is the case with its next manifestation,
'hallucinian via'. It is a hallucination, and the Eleu-

sinia Via, the path followed in the Eleusinian Mysteries.[15] The 'aurellian gape' is the Aurelian Gate of Rome, another burial allusion as it led to the Mausoleum of Hadrian. It is also a sensory pathway, a gaping ear. The Sunken Road is harder to justify in its accepted sense as the *Hohle Gasse* near Kussnacht where William Tell ambushed the tyrant Gessler.[18] Then there is a grassgrown track, along which to trek, that has grown gross. The 'crimeslaved cruxway' is partly a real path, constructed by criminal slaves, and partly a *via crucis,* a mystical way of the Stations of the Cross, which Joyce in fact said was a pattern represented in the form of Book III.[19] It also sounds vaguely like the 'Giant's Causeway' in Northern Ireland: ᛘ is, of course, a giant. None of these potential paths has materialized, nor is there any sound (moorhen's cry) or gangplank to bring the investigators closer to 'hopenhaven'. As archaeologists exploring a burial mound in Dublin they might well be reaching towards Copenhagen, for Viking remains abound beneath the pavements. But as mystics in pursuit of a hope of heaven they are confounded by Yawn's French, the language of Malherbe.[20] Is such the whence-(it)-is-derived (Latin, *unde derivatur*)[15] matter of the case, monsieur? Is such the original content of the casemate, the chamber in the mound? Frankly, (*quo*) *magis enarratur* (*eo*) *minus hoc intellego*, the more completely it is explained the less I understand this.[15]

'How?', replies Yawn, translating French *comment.* '*C'est mal prononçable*', it is hard for his questioners to pronounce. They stutter (Italian, *tartagliano*)[21] their French (Spanish, *Francés*). To the one who has just spoken he exclaims '*Vous n'avez pas d'eau dans votre bouche provinciale, monsieur*', you have no water in your provincial mouth, sir. The mispronounced words sound to him like German (*Boche*) or Provençal. '*Je m'incline, mais moi, j'ai trouvé la clef dans les champs*', I acquiesce, but me, I've found the key in the fields. He's found the path there too, not only *la clef* but also German *Klee,* shamrock.[22] '*Et ça n'a pas de valure*', and that has no value. '*Comment*?' This contradiction, that the shamrock merely represents the Trinity, and is valueless in itself, completes the bewilderment of Yawn's audience.

We saw in our first example that certain very diverse human beings were incorporated in the character ⋔ . In the second example he also included inanimate objects, mountains. Now, we must appreciate that FW also employs entirely inanimate conglomerates which are formed in the same way. The story in the first example, the 'farce of dustiny', was found to include a drama of Caesar's death, a model of Vico's philosophy, and the text of FW itself. From numerous examples throughout the book, we can state definitively that the burial mound we have just discussed, and the letter which is unearthed from it, are both part of the same complex amalgam, which further includes all Wakean notions of buildings and cities. These things are ultimately containers of ⋔ , and whether they are real containers of his body or verbal containers of his name they are indifferently represented in Joyce's manuscripts by the siglum ☐ . The language predicament of the four old men—they

blame the language and its speaker blames their pro-
nunciation—is often our problem when we attempt to
impale ⊓ in the labyrinth of FW. The more ☐ is
narrated the less we understand. It is this container
concept ☐ which is invoked in our Book IV excerpt
(597.04-22):

> Of all the stranger things that ever not even in the
> hundrund and badst pageans of unthowsent and wonst
> nice or in eddas and oddes bokes of tomb, dyke and
> hollow to be have happened! The untireties of livesliving
> being the one substrance of a streamsbecoming. Totalled
> in toldteld and teldtold in tittletell tattle. Why? Be-
> cause, graced be Gad and all giddy gadgets, in whose
> words were the beginnings, there are two signs to turn
> to, the yest and the ist, the wright side and the wronged
> side, feeling aslip and wauking up, so an, so farth. Why?
> On the sourdsite we have the Moskiosk Djinpalast with
> its twin adjacencies, the bathouse and the bazaar,
> allahallahallah, and on the sponthesite it is the alcovan
> and the rosegarden, boony noughty, all puraputhry.
> Why? One's apurr apuss a story about brid and break-
> fedes and parricombating and coushcouch but others is
> of tholes and oubworn buyings, dolings and chafferings
> in heat, contest and enmity. Why? Every talk has his
> stay, vidnis Shavarsanjivana, and all-a-dreams perhapsing
> under lucksloop at last are through. Why? It is a sot of a
> swigswag, systomy dystomy, which everabody you ever
> anywhere at all doze. Why? Such me.

To a degree, FW is supposed to illustrate the
activity of the sleeping mind, and Book IV portrays
that mind in the process of awakening. At this point
the three preceding Books appear in retrospect as the
dissolving dream. Of all the strangest things that did
not even happen in the hundred and one worst pages

of *A Thousand and One Nights,* or in odds and ends
of the Icelandic *Eddas* or the Egyptian *Book of the
Dead* !

This passage exhibits a common Wakean idio-
syncrasy. Its words are often susceptible to two alter-
native constructions which contradict one another,
the so-called 'identity of opposites' discussed by the
medieval philosopher Giordano Bruno. For instance
'badst' ought to mean worst, most bad, but it sounds
rather like 'best'. If we view the *Arabian Nights* as an
unholy book, full of pagans, and possibly 'not sent by
thou', the former construction applies. Alternatively
we have the hundred best pages of a 'nice' book: the
night is over and has been won ('wonst'). We should
also heed the symmetrical pairing of elements in these
sentences: 'badst' is opposed to 'wonst'. The ambivalent syntax, e.g. 'to be have happened', widening
the connotative spectrum, is also a typical Book IV
trademark.

The odd books of 'tomb, dyke and hollow' remind
us of documents concealed in tumuli, but readers
slightly familiar with the rest of FW will probably
also perceive the names of Tom, Dick and Harry. This
triad relates, for instance, to Brutus, Antony and
Cassius in Book I, and both are technically embodi-
ments of the sigla ∧ , ⊄ and ⊏ .

The dreamer is enthralled to see that all the untir-
ing entities of life's living were made the one sub-
stance, in his trance, of a stream of verbalization. To
gloss 'streamsbecoming' we could notice the subsequent 'in whose words were the beginnings' and
quote Leo Knuth on another variant of that phrase:

As it says in the book: 'In the becoming was the weared' (FW 487.20). The matrix of this sentence is obvious. The opening words of the gospel according to St John are a recurrent motif. We see that 'weared' means 'word': the Logos. Phonetically it also suggests 'weird'—a suggestion which is semantically supported by the word 'becoming', because that is what 'weird' originally meant: OE *wyrd*, the power to which everything is subjected, the power that causes everything to become, time (past, present and future) and change (which is merely an aspect of time). Man is born, lives, and dies in time, 'dreeing his weird' (FW 199.05). *Wyrd* is cognate with German *werden* (auxiliary of the passive and the future) and with Dutch *worden* (to become).[23]

The 'streamsbecoming' totalled life's entireties, and was told in tittle-tattle, in petty gossip. The dreamer questions its purpose and learns that, by the grace of God and of material things (gadgets), it has two sides to turn to, a form literally illustrated in 'toldteld and teldtold'. There is a West side, falling asleep with the setting sun, and an East side, waking up. The 'yest' is yesterday, the past, opposed to the present tense (German *ist*, is).[24] But these definitions are ambivalent, the right side being not only constructed by a rightful God but also by a human wright, and the wrong side also being wronged, i.e. in the right. □ , as we generally observe in FW, 'has its cardinal points' (114.07), and there are also a South and a North side. The South side features the Great Mosque at Mecca prior to Mohammed: it is full of djinns and devils, and incorporates the profane bath-house (and bathouse!) and bazaar. Bloom of course visits 'the mosque of the baths' on the South side of Dublin just before 'Hades', not hell perhaps but a contrast to the post-Mohammed 'sponthesite' with its Koran and rosegarden. However, ambivalence triumphs: the South side is also North, as it includes the Moscow gin palace (German *Palast*, palace)[24], and it is further the energetic bazaar of waking existence, with morning prayers to Allah, as opposed to the paradise of dreams (Italian, *buena notte*, goodnight)[25] I do not understand why the South side is deaf (French, *sourd*), but presumably some balancing ingredient exists in 'sponthesite'. I suppose 'puraputhry' and 'apurr apuss' might echo 'purpose' - the dreamer's current preoccupation—but the cat seems to be here just to match the dog in the next answer.

The 'apurr apuss' answer is a sort of inversion of the 'sourdsite' one. Again it has two contrasting parts, but now the first is the dream, i.e. the previous three Books of FW, and the second is the hell of reality. 'Once upon a time', the opening words of Joyce's *Portrait*, might be taken to represent birth, the characteristic institution of Vico's first age, when man sought shelter in caves (bed and breakfast). Book II contains the parricide of the Russian General and the fighting on equal terms (Italian, *combattere ad armi pari*)[25] of his two sons. Book III is the period of sleep (French, *se coucher*), ocurring after twelve midnight, which chimes at its opening (FW 403).

The future side is less comfortable. We will have to thole, to endure, the hardships of buying, dealing and chaffering in heat, contest and enmity. The English word 'chaffer' means to trade or barter, but 'chaffering' sounds rather like 'suffering'. Noticing Humphrey

Chimpden Earwicker's initials in the last words we again ask why, but the dream is sliding out of focus. Every dog has his day, witness Shavarsanjivana. If we can trust the late B.P. Misra[26], this is a book in the Purva Mimamsa school of Indian philosophy. The Purva Mimamsa ('first inquiry') scholars did not accept the existence of God, but thought the Vedas were eternal and uncreated, and devoted themselves to their interpretation. Perhaps there is a parallel in the recommended approach to the text of FW. Anyway, the stream of the Liffey, now passing Leixlip, or else under the Loop Line railway bridge, nears the sea, into which it will plunge on the closing page of FW. The terminal image of ◻ is simply that of its antitheses, systole and diastole. Dozing and waking are activities undertaken by everyone you ever saw. Why? Search me. That isn't the sort of question FW is there to answer.

2
Learning to read
FINNEGANS WAKE

I come from a fairly boring place in the South of England. From an early age I was attracted by black magic, and it eventually struck me that an acquaintance with spiders would be a desirable asset. From spending most of my time with my numerous pet spiders I became gradually committed to the study of biology, and I proceded to extend my enthusiasm to longhorned grasshoppers and acellular slime fungi. I had already streamed into the sciences at school when I began reading Joyce in the autumn of 1963.

It was not until I was about 200 pages into *Ulysses* that the cumulative effect reached me. From my first exposure to Joyce I remember vividly how strangely familiar I found some of his observations. For instance in the opening chapter of *A Portrait of the Artist as a Young Man,* Stephen opens and closes the flaps of his ears, thinking about the sound of a train in a tunnel. I knew that association at once from experience. In *Ulysses* he perceives that certain gestures of his have been unconsciously imitated from other people. As he lies back on the rocks he thinks 'That is Kevin Egan's movement I made nodding for his nap'[1]. Smiling in the library he thinks 'Smile.

Smile Cranly's smile.'[2] Some months before reading
this I had discovered that I did the same sort of thing,
but it hadn't occurred to me that such behavioural
niceties could be documented.

Initial contact with *Ulysses* was an extremely
personal sensation and it took me some time to
acknowledge that this writer had so much potential
interest that I could not afford to ignore him. I was
aware that there was another step beyond *Ulysses*,
but it was not until June 1964 that I felt ready to
look at *Finnegans Wake*, aware already of its reputed
impenetrability.

Opening the book, I read slowly and mechanically
as far as page 18, where I reached the lines '(Stoop)
. . . to this claybook . . . Can you rede (since We and
Thou had it out already) its world?' I closed it. I felt
that I had made a respectable attempt and that I
could not read its world. Or at least, the results of so
doing were paltry compared with the cascade of
illumination pouring out of *Ulysses*, so I returned to
the earlier work. The first reading had taken two
weeks. The second took two months and I continued
reading *Ulysses* intermittently for the rest of the
year.

Essentially, my early impressions were forms of
recognition: I identified with the voice of the interior
monologue. The things which seemed important to
Joyce seemed important to me, and I found the
moods and situations charged with a penetrating
timeless sanctity. *Ulysses* looks very closely at a
mediocre day in a mediocre setting. Using a massive
reservoir of exotic effects it endows this day with a

corona of wonder and significance. At the same time it retains the sense of realism by photographing numerous trivial objects normally seen only from the corner of the eye. It taught me to observe my own surroundings with greater care. But *Ulysses* possesses a preordained wellspring of sanctity in so far as its protagonist unconsciously re-enacts the adventures of the Homeric wanderer. Surely Joyce's motive in having him do this was to intimate a timeless pattern underlying ostensibly capricious events? I didn't exactly *believe* in such patterns, but I liked the idea of them.

As I read on I became increasingly conscious of the astonishing beauty of Joyce's phrasing, and the obvious care which had been taken in creating it. The general axiom seemed to be 'brevity objectivises'. For Joyce, to fuse words rather than to hyphenate them is to engender new tangible entities. For instance, in the first chapter 'oakpale', 'grasshalms', 'musk-perfumed', 'ghostcandle'. Or in the third ('Proteus'):

> Under its leaf he watched through peacocktwittering lashes the southing sun. I am caught in this burning scene. Pan's hour, the faunal noon. Among gumheavy serpentplants, milkoozing fruits, where on the tawny waters leaves lie wide. Pain is far.[3]

Of course, I was confronted by unexplained allusions on every page, but I was able to tolerate this, for the allusions I could explain were quite enough to cope with for the moment. I began to read authors of whom Joyce approved, such as Ibsen and Flaubert, in search of further insight, but I felt a strong aversion to examining any critical study. I did not wish to have a third party intervene between my awareness and the reality of which it was aware.

Each of the eighteen chapters of *Ulysses* is written in a different style. The final and most gratifying effect produced by it was a kind of unified concept-ualising of the style of each chapter. I could see a per-manent yet ineffable quality radiating from each block of colour, and I appreciated the balance of these eighteen distinct qualities against one another. What I would eventually discover was that this same principle operates in FW.

In the spring of 1965 I was at Imperial College, London, studying for a BSc in zoology and entomol-ogy. I was a member of the British Spider Study Group and vaguely contemplating a career in research into spider behaviour. During the Easter break I made my first visit to Dublin, specifically to examine the topography of *Ulysses*. Having got off the boat, I was taken by bus to Pearse Street (Great Brunswick Street in Joyce's time), to the region where the 'Lotus-Eaters' episode occurs. The weather was hot and the dull brown houses made me think of stage-scenery. 'In Westland Row he halted before the window of the Belfast and Oriental Tea Company and read the legends of leadpapered packets: choice blend, finest quality, family tea. Rather warm. Tea . . . . He turned into Cumberland street and, going on some paces, halted in the lee of the station wall. No-one. Meade's timberyard. Piled balks. Ruins and tenements. With careful tread he passed over a hopscotch court with its forgotten pickeystone. Not a sinner. Near the

timberyard a squatted child at marbles alone, shooting the taw with a cunnythumb. A wise tabby, a
blinking sphinx, watched from her warm sill. Pity to
disturb them.'[4]

It is not strange that some older people in Dublin
think of *Ulysses* as a homely sort of book, a nostalgia
trip. It became clear to me that I had not tasted its
true essence before visiting the warm pavements of
Westland Row, the harsh bright seascape of Sandy-
mount and the abrupt tranquillity of Howth Head. I
was acutely conscious of my ignorance both of Irish
culture and of Joyce's own life in the city. When I
returned to London I read a history of Ireland and
also began Ellmann's biography, *James Joyce*, but I
was obliged to stop when Ellmann spoke of the composition of FW. I was determined to avoid other
people's viewpoints, although I did notice from
Ellmann that 'Finnegan's Wake' was the title of a
song, and I copied out its wording from his version.

It was becoming inevitable that I would attempt
FW and I felt that since first looking at it I had been
conserving my psychological assets in anticipation of
the task. I made a new start in the summer. My
technique was slightly fanatical. I was so anxious to
capture the undistorted experience that on reaching
page 29, where the first chapter ends, I tied a thread
round all the remaining pages to prevent my accident-
ally looking ahead. Every few months there would be
a solemn undoing of the thread: I would read a new
chapter and then tie up the remaining ones. It took
two and a half years to reach the end of FW.

Having initially read through any chapter I would

spend a week or two repeating the process and then make a frontal assault with dictionaries. My knowledge of foreign languages was not impressive. We had done some French and Latin at school but I knew virtually no German or Italian and it was clear that Joyce exploited both of these languages continually. I would take a dictionary and work through the chapter, looking up any word I thought suited the language in question. I soon learned that the most cryptic elements were often pure English. Grotesque orthography was often repeated verbatim in the Oxford English Dictionary. I suspected that Joyce was deliberately revivifying many archaic and dialectical usages. Partridge's *Dictionary of Slang and Unconventional English* and the *Oxford Dictionary of English Proverbs* provided numerous identifications of items in FW or of words very close to Joyce's.

As well as common words, thousands of personal names turn up, and I filled a notebook with an alphabetical listing of these, which I then checked against the *Dictionary of National Biography* and several international biographical dictionaries. Some characters were so important that I felt obliged to read separate studies of them, notably Swift, Parnell, Lewis Carroll and Giordano Bruno. Bruno was the consequence of my examining *The Critical Writings of James Joyce*, which I assumed would be harmless as it consists chiefly of early work. But it includes Joyce's review of a book on Bruno, and I was caught out by a footnote to this: 'Coleridge anticipated Joyce's interest in both Bruno and Vico'[5]. The name of Vico was unknown to me, but I decided that the

only sensible course was to look at the philosophy
shelves, and I accordingly located *The New Science*
and Croce's biography of Vico. The relevance of both
was soon clear.

By October 1965 I had digested the first four
chapters of FW (up to 103) and I paused to revise the
material so far covered. I was not enjoying the process very much. A great many definitions and odd
little facts had accumulated, but they didn't really
make the text cohere. Chapters 1, 3 and 4 all proceeded jerkily from subject to subject. For instance,
the original point on FW 18 where I had stopped the
previous year coincides with a sudden change of
context (which partly caused my stopping). Before
this point, we have heard a dialogue between 'Mutt'
and 'Jute' about a burial mound:

> Mutt. — . . . Now are all tombed to the mound, isges to
>   isges, erde from erde. Pride, O pride, thy prize!
> Jute. — 'Stench!
> Mutt. — Fiatfuit! Hereinunder lyethey . . . in this sound
>   seemetery which iz leebez luv.

It ends as follows:

> Mutt. — Ore you astoneaged, jute you?
> Jute. — Oye am thonthorstrok, thing mud.

The words 'thing mud' suggesting the Thingmote, the
Viking assembly in ancient Dublin, which took place
on a kind of conical mound. The next sentence is the
one I quoted earlier, exhorting the reader to stoop to
a 'claybook', and leads to a two-page account of the
origins of the alphabet and of printing. I can now
explain the transition by observing that the text

adheres faithfully to its real subject, the container siglum ◻ , but I had no conception of such things at this stage. I noticed words from the song about Finnegan's Wake in chapter 1 but I was surprised to find the subject dropped when I reached chapter 2.

I.2 (as it is conventionally represented) was far easier to read than I.1. It was a story about a man called H.C. Earwicker. The text explained that he acquired the name Earwicker when a visiting king made a joke about earwigs, and proceeds to sketch his encounter with 'a cad with a pipe' in the Phoenix Park, who asks him the time. Earwicker reacts by defending his reputation, which suggests immediately that he is in some way guilty, and the cad later repeats his words. They pass from person to person, eventually reaching 'Hosty', who is thereby inspired to compose 'The Ballad of Persse O'Reilly', which closes the chapter.

I.2 is followed by two chapters which I found uninteresting and rather similar. The narrative led nowhere: I was merely given an array of different people's opinions of Earwicker, all of them very diverse and inconsistent. The prospect of the rest of FW being perhaps equally unprofitable made me contemplate giving up the endeavour, but luckily I.5 made more sense, being moulded in a simpler language.

I.5 is an account of ◻ as a letter or document, and also as FW itself. I was perfectly able to see that the letter was FW. Joyce, for example, doesn't use inverted commas to distinguish speech, and the narrator contemplates 'inferring from the nonpresence of inverted commas (sometimes called quotation marks) on any page that its author was always constitutionally incapable of misappropriating the spoken words of others' (108.33-6). In fact, Joyce did spend a lot of time overhearing conversations and then working them in to his productions, as I knew from Ellmann's biography.

I.5 seemed to me a sort of defence or apology for FW, advising the prospective reader 'Now, patience; and remember patience is the great thing' (108.08). Sure. But I thought a careful consideration of I.5 would eventually explain the rationale of FW. It doesn't. Its narrator simply voices the average reader's bewilderment in a pedestrian style, and had I been less desperate for philosophical remuneration I would have distinguished the narrator's sentiments from those of Joyce. Tantalizing hints ended in impasses, for instance 119.17-27: 'the meant to be baffling chrismon trilithon sign m, finally called after some his hes hecitency Hec, which, moved contrawatchwise, represents his title in sigla . . . why not take the former for a village inn. . . ?'

It might be interesting to examine a I.5 paragraph as an illustration of the simplest form the FW text can take. Few sections of the book are as immediately comprehensible as, say the following:

> I am a worker, a tombstone mason, anxious to pleace averyburies and jully glad when Christmas comes his once ayear. You are a poorjoist, unctuous to polise nopebobbies and tunnibelly soully when 'tis thime took o'er home, gin. We cannot say aye to aye. We cannot smile noes from noes. Still. One cannot help noticing that rather more than half of the lines run north-south in

the Nemzes and Bukarahast directions while the others
go west-east in search from Maliziies with Bulgarad for,
tiny tot though it looks when schtschupnistling alongside other incunabula, it has its cardinal points for all
that. These ruled barriers along which the traced words,
run, march, halt, walk, stumble at doubtful points,
stumble up again in comparative safety seem to have
been drawn first of all in a pretty checker with lamp-
black and blackthorn. Such crossing is antechristian of
course, but the use of the homeborn shillelagh as an aid
to calligraphy shows a distinct advance from savagery to
barbarism. It is seriously believed by some that the intention may have been geodetic, or, in the view of the
cannier, domestic economical. But in writing thithaways
end to end and turning, turning and end to end hithaways writing and with lines of litters slittering up and
louds of latters slettering down, the old semetomyplace
and jupetbackagain from tham Let Rise till Hum Lit.
Sleep, where in the waste is the wisdom? (113.34-114.
20)

When I first read this I could at least appreciate
that it was a description of a piece of writing. But I
failed to identify the 'I' and 'you' who are in dispute.
I assumed 'I' was Joyce telling the reader, 'you', that
he, Joyce, was a worker. I can now see that the word
'poorjoist' is an amalgam of Joyce's name with the
word 'bourgeois': the official Communist critic would
regard Joyce as a 'bourgeois' writer. It is therefore the
'you' of the passage which actually denotes Joyce.
The narrator, 'I', is a Communist worker, a peaceful
employee in the funeral industry, anxious to please
everybody, and jolly glad when 'Christmas comes but
once a year'. He appreciates a holiday: Lord Avebury
introduced the English bank holidays, and Danish *jul*
means 'Christmas'.[6] Joyce, on the other hand, is a

bourgeois, relying on the police to hold the mob from his door. He is anxious to please nobody. With his continual late-night indulgence in the fruits of decadence he is always terribly sorry when it's time to go home again. The epithet 'tunbelly', used in *Ulysses* to acknowledge the reputed obesity of St Thomas Aquinas,[7] is not appropriate to Joyce, but then the description of him is clearly biassed: it is true that he drank too much, but the drink in question was not gin.

Joyce and his critic cannot see eye to eye or smell nose from nose. I looked up 'noes' in the Shorter Oxford and found a word 'noesis', defined as '*a*. The sum-total of the mental action of a rational animal. *b*. An intellectual view of the moral and physical world.' Clearly, bourgeois and Communist differ not solely in their interpretations of sensory data but also in their modes of intellection. Still, says the text, they cannot but agree that about half of the lines in the object they are contemplating run north-south while the others go west-east.

I did not, of course, know that there was an Albanian cluster here, including such words as *Nemc* (= Austrian, German), *búkur* (= beautiful), *rahat* (= quiet) and *mali* (= mountain).[8] I could see Bucharest and Belgrade but not Malaysia. The places didn't bother me so much as the need to justify this equation of the book or letter with a map, possessing cardinal points. The 'schtschup. . . ' prevented my apprehending that it was *nestling* alongside other incunabula, but the Shorter Oxford defined this latter term as 'books produced in the infancy of printing', confirming that the writing under discussion was indeed some old book.

I think I realised after a while that 'such crossing is antechristian' meant that the crosses produced by the checkerwork of lines were not to be taken as Christian Crosses but as something older, but the concept of writing with a shillelagh (blackthorn stick) was lost on me. I now appreciate the intimation that an ancient Irish writer of the Finn MacCool period, had such a person existed, would be a physical giant, and be obliged to use an elephantine writing instrument. 'Geodetic' means 'pertaining to surveying', so we have marks made on the ground with a stick, intermediate in nature between a map and a missive. The key to the concept, of course, is again ◘ , as simultaneously a book and an edifice. My classical learning had not developed to the point of recognizing 'economical' as deriving from Greek *oikonomikos*, which means the same thing as Latin *domesticus*, 'pertaining to the house'.[9]

I knew I.1 well enough to remember 005.03-4, 'with larrons o'toolers clittering up and tombles a'buckets clottering down', which is echoed near the end of the passage. But according to O Hehir and Dillon,[9] the earlier part of the sentence, 'writing thithaways . . . hithaways writing', alludes to the *boustrophêdon*, a method of writing alternate lines from left to right and from right to left, as in some ancient inscriptions. Obviously this horizontal process is contrasted with the vertical one as an extension of the crossing concept.

I could just about see Noah's sons Shem, Ham

in FW), and I guessed that 'semetomyplace' might be 'cemetery-place': death contrasted with resurrection (jumping back again). 'Let Rise' must be a point in the rude past where letters, the alphabet, arose, and as such contrasts with the modern age of Humane Letters, (Hum.Lit., *Humaniores Literae*[9]). So in this succession of writings from the past to the present, says the narrator, where exactly is the wisdom? I thought he was going to tell me.

My progress through FW was characterized by paroxysms of enthusiasm for some element in the text which seemed of paramount urgency when discovered, but which gave way to some totally different enthusiasm a few months later. In December I read Blake's *Jerusalem*, knowing from the account in *Critical Writings* that Joyce approved of Blake. Suddenly I perceived the analogy between the sleep of Albion and that of Finnegan. Both were giants and both were emotionally involved with two women. That type of relationship could also be found in Swift, in Ibsen's heroes such as the Master Builder, and even in Jesus with Martha and Mary, which Bloom recalls occasionally in the context of his own dual relationship with Martha Clifford and Molly. It seemed for a time that FW was all about Blake, but then my enthusiasm shifted, first to Le Fanu's *The House by the Churchyard*[10] and then to Madame Blavatsky's *Isis Unveiled*.

It was becoming clear that Finnegan and Earwicker were very much the same person, and I.6 reinforced this impression. In fact this chapter was the most important turning-point in my experience: after

absorbing it I was totally committed to going on with
FW. It is divided into twelve questions, each consider-
ing a fundamental personage in the *Wake*, and attri-
butes of both Finnegan and Earwicker blend in
question 1 (126.10-139.14; my italics):

> 1. What secondtonone myther rector and maximost
> bridgesmaker was the first to rise taller through his
> beanstale . . . *h*allucination, *c*auchman, *e*ctoplasm . . . is
> an *e*xcrescence to *c*ivilised *h*umanity . . . blows whisk-
> ery around his summit but stehts stout upon his footles;
> stutters fore he falls and goes mad entirely when he's
> waked; is Timb to the pearly morn and Tomb to the
> mourning night; and an he had the best bunbaked bricks
> in bould Babylon for his pitching plays he'd be lost for
> the want of his wan wubblin wall?
>   Answer: Finn MacCool!

This question 1 was tedious, but in question
11 (148.33-168.12) I saw what appeared to be a
deeper continuation of the I.5 philosophical defence
of the book. I spent a lot of time in London walking
about pondering sentences like 'What the romantic in
rags pines after like all tomtompions haunting crev-
ices for a deadbeat escupement . . . is the poorest
commononguardiant waste of time . . . I fail to see
when . . . while, for aught I care to the contrary, the
all is *where*' (151.17-36).[11]
   Still confident that this expressed Joyce's apology
for FW, I formulated a theory of his rejection of
romanticism and time. Joyce is a supremely classical
artist: he rationally refines each detail of his work,
and in scrutinizing the whole edifice at a glance he
ensures that those details cohere. A romantic artist
would work intuitively, conscious at any time only of

what was being put down then. Joyce, who cared little for contemporary world events, would surely prefer space, the eternal *where,* illustrated by his locating FW in Dublin, to time, the transient *when* of the man who lives solely in the present. Thus FW blends elements from all periods of history with assured indifference.

This theory happens to be totally fallacious. Unfortunately it took me a long time to discover that, and when I did discover it I felt that one of the foundation-blocks had been violently dislodged. I could of course appreciate that Shem, the artist, in chapter I.7, was a portrait of Joyce, and I also appreciated that he was linked to time rather than to space, but I ignored the contradiction until the autumn of 1968. At that point Adaline Glasheen drew my attention to a letter in which Joyce states that he based the narrator of question 11 on his enemy Wyndham Lewis.[12] Mrs Glasheen eventually demonstrated[13] that the question was full of the titles of Lewis's works.

Lewis's *Time and Western Man* is really the key to the question, but on account of my solitary technique I hadn't heard of it. It contains a hysterical and illconsidered attack on *Ulysses* as being an expression of 'the Philosophy of time'. Hence Joyce makes Lewis a representative of opposing space, deriding the romantic escapists such as himself.

The energy and enthusiasm I acquired from my false theory sustained my progress with the reading until the close of Book I, which I reached in July 1966. After some general revision of the Book, I departed on a university expedition to Western Nigeria to collect acellular slime fungi (Myxomycetes). These are inconspicuous organisms, half plant and half animal, found principally under pieces of water-logged timber on the forest floor. There is a certain parallel between the collection of Myxomycetes and the exegesis of FW. In both cases the trick is to acquire an instinct for the potentially most profitable areas to search. A forest contains an infinitude of logs and twigs, and the spongier they are, the better their chance of supporting Myxomycetes. Unless you are able to predict whilst upright which sticks will repay your turning them over, you'll wear yourself out on unproductive material. At the same time some part of one's consciousness should monitor the rest of the environment, because there will always be certain treasures concealed in unexpected niches.

At intervals during the expedition I read the first and second chapters of Book II. As I explained earlier, this is extremely obscure, and the first chapter failed to impress me at the time, despite its weird twilit sexuality. But II.2 provoked my sympathy on first contact. I was intrigued by the eccentric layout—footnotes and two sets of marginal notes—and the language was especially picturesque. For instance 274.23-5: 'the sparksown fermament of the starryk fieldgosongingon where blows a nemone at each blink of windstill'. I felt a measure of familiarity with the geometry jargon of the latter part of the chapter, which made its eventual resolution seem feasible. Consider 283.32-284.14:

Show that the median, hce che ech, interecting at royde

angles the parilegs of a given obtuse one biscuts both the arcs that are in curveachord behind. Brickbaths. The family umbroglia. A Tullagrove pole to the Height of County Fearmanagh has a septain inclinaison and the graphplot for all the functions in Lower County Monachan, whereat samething is rivisible by nighttim, may be involted into the zeroic couplet, palls pell inhis heventh glike noughty times ∞ , find, if you are not literally cooefficient, how minney combinaisies and permutandies can be played on the international surd!

The footnotes often possess a demented childishness, e.g. 271.F2: 'Skip one, flop fore, jennies in the cabbage store', or else they offer fatuous pseudoglosses. 265.F2, on 'brandnewburgher', gives 'A viking vernacular expression still used in the Summerhill district for a jerryhatted man of forty who puts two fingers into his boiling soupplate and licks them in turn to find out if there is enough mushroom catsup in the mutton broth.'

II.2 is composed of paragraphs, each of which bears a heading in the right-hand margin, such as 'GNOSIS OF PRECREATE DETERMINATION. AGNOSIS OF POSTCREATE DETERMINISM.' (262.R2) or 'ARCHAIC ZELOTYPIA AND THE ODIUM TELEOLOGICUM' (264.R1). I decided that my priority was to relate headings to paragraphs so that a serial progression might be discerned. I see now that most of my conclusions were somewhat naive. But they kept me entranced until November, when I untied the thread enclosing II.3. This is a very long chapter (309-382) and its characters interact considerably, supplying an element I had missed in Book

I. But it is ludicrously difficult to sort out the cast, relate them to the rest of FW, and understand what they say to each other. The extract we looked at earlier, with the Rhaeto-Romanic, is absolutely typical. Ellmann's biography contained two anecdotes of Joyce's father which provide the framework for much of II.3—the tailor who makes a suit of clothes for the Norwegian Captain, and Buckley who shoots the Russian General[14] —but it was years before I conceded that one did not need to know the anecdotes beforehand, that they could in fact be intuited from the text.

1967 was the year of my finals and the combination of that distraction with the prodigious difficulties of II.3 restrained me until March, when I rapidly absorbed the short II.4 and reached the end of Book II. About this time I began reading the abridged edition of Frazer's *The Golden Bough*, and found my enthusiasm once again buoyed up. I could see that the fall of Finnegan, the disgrace of Earwicker and the shooting of the Russian General all illustrated the ritual murder of the divine king. Frazer's synthesis of world mythology slid smoothly on to Joyce's template. FW was beginning to look far more archetypal than I had suspected.[15]

I assumed that the tension would continue to grow as I entered Book III; instead, I found its first two chapters rather lax. There was much decoration, but the basic sentiments of the characters were rather transparent. III.1 featured a stage-Irish postman named Shaun, based, it turned out, on a character in the works of the Irish playwright Dion Boucicault.[16]

III.2 provided an obvious variant in a parish priest named Jaun. I assumed, when I began III.3 in September, that the person there named Yawn was a third variant.

The names Shem and Shaun are often paired opposites in FW, for instance at the close of Book I: 'Who were Shem and Shaun the living sons or daughters of?' But it is more convenient to reserve the name Shaun for the III.1 protagonist, and Shem for the I.7 protagonist. Joyce's manuscript sigla can be used to represent the totality of the opposed qualities: I did not know of these at the time, but I could see that the Book III protagonists were connected. They are variants of ∧, as opposed to ⊏. Although I could not define the sigla, I could recognize their presence, and it will simplify my argument if I continue to use them.

I found the early parts of III.3 very individual and often rich in a bright outdoor imagery, but after 532 the style changed. The chapter closed with twenty-two pages of long pedantic paragraphs: a speech by ⋔. As ⋔ had been prominent in the first half of Book I. I assumed this was his return to occupy the stage until the close of Book III. This would be in keeping with the ⊏ /∧ balance of the other halves of those Books.

I was becoming impatient to reach the end of FW and the tone of this speech aggravated my impatience. III.4, a portrait of ⋔'s family life, bored me. What I had not expected was the short undivided Book IV, which I did not discover until December. By this stage my ability to memorise the text seemed to be in decline, and I still find, twelve years later, that the last hundred pages of FW are the part I know least well. It was only after some months of pondering that I decided the primary function of Book IV must be as a counterweight to Book II rather than to I.1.

Having left Imperial College far too obsessed with FW to think seriously about a career, I started making tentative visits to professional zoologists, including a Mr Broughton, with whom I shared an interest in longhorned grasshoppers (bush crickets, *Tettigoniidae*). He asked in conversation whether I would care to take up a studentship in an animal acoustics laboratory outside Paris. The prospect sounded very appealing: a sound knowledge of French would improve my understanding of FW, and as the book had been written in Paris, there was an obvious incentive to get to know the place.

Immediately before leaving England I reached the end of FW. At last I was going to be able to examine other people's pronouncements on the subject. I felt rather affected by the pathos of the closing monologue but that sort of thing passes off pretty quickly. I packed a number of books on FW and got on the boat.

3
Other people's opinions

I don't like general introductions to Joyce. As Anthony Farrow said in a review, 'The heavy, scholastic fog of the *a priori* trails along their pages, and these critics with their 'epiphanies' and their *'claritas'* have done almost as much to make Joyce difficult as the sage of Zurich himself.'[1] The writers of general introductions must take responsibility for the common misconception that Joycean scholarship is largely concerned with demonstrating *symbols*. Robert Adams gives an illustration which is good enough to quote at length:

> One of Mr Bloom's gayest family memories is of a trip he took with Milly around the Kish lighthouse on a boat called the *Erin's King*. Everyone else was sick and scared, because of the rough weather, but not Milly; Bloom recalls with warm paternal affection her pale blue scarf loose in the wind with her hair, and thinks also of how he gave stale cake to the seagulls. Among earnest readers of *Ulysses*, the name of the vessel has given rise to some determined symbol searching. Erin, to be sure, had many kings in the historic past from Partholon to Roderick O' Connor. But Parnell was known as Ireland's uncrowned king—to Mrs O'Shea, more effusively, as Her Own King— and Joyce's particular devotion in politics (verb-

ally, at least) was to Parnell. Thus the name of the boat has been supposed to involve a transient, poignant recollection of Parnell. (As a matter of fact, by documentary accident, we know that Joyce had Parnell in mind here and intended Bloom to be aware of Parnell too; a notesheet for 'Eumaeus' in the British Museum includes the phrase 'LB never forget trip on Erin's King (C.S.P.).' But, setting aside this positive knowledge, which we possess only by accident, let us consider the passage in itself.) A first oddity about the reference to Parnell is that it is most apparent to a reader who is not well acquainted with turn-of-the-century Dublin. Most of Joyce's symbols work quite the other way; they imply some knowledge of the social milieu. But the reader to whom the name *Erin's King* most forcefully suggests Parnell is the one who does not know it was a real boat, the only boat one could take on an expedition of this nature. Just as Bloom recalls, it was an old tub; it plied from Custom House Quay during summer months, taking tourists for a shilling a head around Ireland's Eye or around the Kish lighthouse. On the occasion of regattas in Dublin Bay, it sometimes took people out to watch the races. Advertisements indicating its schedule appeared regularly in the *Freeman's Journal* and other papers during the 1890's. If Bloom had chosen to recall a brief two-hour excursion by water (and one of the points about Bloom is that he has travelled widely in Dublin), he could have sailed on no other vessel than the *Erin's King*. If Joyce had any respect at all for the surface texture of his facts—and the available evidence indicates that details of this sort were of passionate interest to him—he could have given the boat no other name.

Of course the really earnest symbol-seeker will urge that the mere physical existence of a boat by this name does not detract from its symbolic significance. Joyce (like his readers) found in the world without, as actual, what was already in his world within, as possible. Thus, if one's mind runs on Parnell, there is every justifiable reason to see the *Erin's King* as a Parnell symbol. Its being an old tub is a symbol of the degradation of Parnell's name; Bloom's feeding the gulls off it is a symbol of humanitarian impulses associated with Parnellism; and Milly's youthful fearlessness in facing the open sea of vital political action is contrasted with the craven cowerings of the average Irishman. This is all arrant nonsense, to be sure, and no one with a grain of common sense would accept it for a minute. But once we are embarked on a symbol search, I can see no reason in theory to disqualify even leaden-footed allegories like this one. Of course we may stipulate that every proposed symbol should serve a demonstrable purpose in the structure of the book or the pattern of our responses to it; but that is a sharp razor indeed, and would probably slice even the basic reference to Parnell out of the passages describing the *Erin's King.*[2]

Distrust of symbols, in reaction to this kind of thing, can reach the point where Fritz Senn takes great care to avoid any use of the word 'symbol' in his Joycean writings. Or as Clive Hart once said to me 'Our lives are full of fucking symbols: we don't need them in our reading matter as well'. What we need, in order to understand Joyce, are reliable facts. For *Ulysses*, most of the available facts are contained in one book, Weldon Thornton's *Allusions in Ulysses*[3]. But until the recent appearance of my *Annotations to Finnegans Wake*[4], the FW situation was extremely untidy. When I arrived in Paris in January 1968, I had with me only part of the factual glossary then in print.

I decided to investigate the literature of FW in a chronological succession, starting with Joyce's own comments in so far as I could obtain them. Some of his letters to his patron, Miss Weaver, include interpretative details, but these are rarely satisfying. For example the word 'violer' on the first page of FW is glossed in a letter of November 1926 'viola in all moods and senses'.[5] This does tell us something about Joyce's attitude: he regarded the meanings of *Wake* words as a potentially infinite series.

More explanations actually originating with Joyce can be found in a collection of essays published in 1929 under the strange title *Our Exagmination Round His Factification for Incamination of Work in Progress*.[6] I met one of the contributors, Stuart Gilbert, in Paris shortly before his death. He told me that he had been given an extract to discuss, and having no idea what it meant, took all his glossary directly from Joyce. Here is an example. For 449.21-4 Joyce has 'till well on into the beausome of the exhaling night, pinching stopandgo jewels out of the hedges and catching dimtop brilliants on the tip of my wagger'. Gilbert's gloss runs:

> *Beausome.* – Suggests *bosom* and *beauty.*
> *Stopandgo jewels.* – Glowworms.
> *Dimtop brilliants.* – He will catch misty dew on the tip of his tongue.[7]

I felt the meaning of 'beausome' was too overt to need stating. The interpretation of 'stopandgo jewels' required more confidence than I had at that stage, but I still fail to see how 'misty dew' accounts for 'dimtop brilliants'. Why doesn't Gilbert explain the point of Jaun's catching dewdrops on his tongue?

Presumably Joyce didn't bother to explain it to him. Most of *Our Exagmination* is so incredibly superficial that it would have done me no harm at all to have read it years earlier. Its authors are Joyce's puppets. Most of it seems designed to thrust FW into the public eye with a barrage of fervent praise. No wonder it didn't sell.

Two other books I had, Connolly's *Scribblede-hobble* and Hayman's *A First Draft Version of Finnegans Wake*, gave me more to think about. They are transcriptions of Joyce's FW manuscripts, and will be considered later in our discussion, but at this juncture they were crucial in showing me sigla in action, and I was thereby enabled to confirm or modify much of my theorizing of the previous year. I had in fact anticipated most of the sigla, and it was gratifying to come upon notes like ' 𝄓 fish x pur et pia belli'[8] (although the transcription is imprecise). I knew that various FW roles were played by a combined ∧ - ⊏ figure, and here I saw his siglum, 𝄓 , connected with a fish, one of his roles.

I now began the famous *Skeleton Key to Finnegans Wake* of Campbell and Robinson. This came out in 1944 and was the first serious attempt to do justice to its subject. It was clearly a more honest appraisal than *Our Exagmination.* Joyce had been dead three years and the authors were enthusiastic American amateurs. As I read the introduction I saw plenty of familiar landmarks: Vico, Tim Finnegan, Finn Mac-Cool, Tristan and Isolde, *The Annals of the Four Masters* and so on. But the curiously literal nature of the interpretation seemed very questionable. Campbell and Robinson's FW was a novel with a plot:

> But to return to HCE. He is a man who has won his place in society, a place not of high distinction but of decent repute. He is a candidate in a local election. Gossip, however, undoes his campaign and his reputation as well. It was in Phoenix Park (that Garden of Eden), near his tavern, that he committed an indecorous impropriety which now dogs him to the end of his life-nightmare. Briefly, he was caught peeping at or exhibiting himself to a couple of girls in Phoenix Park. The indiscretion was witnessed by three drunken soldiers...[9]

And so on. Now, most of this draws on I.2, which is written in a much simpler language than most of FW and is especially amenable to paraphrase. It is true that 034.12-30 gives roughly the same story as Campbell and Robinson: 'Slander ... has never been able to convict ... Earwicker ... of any graver impropriety than that, advanced by some woodwards or regarders, who did not dare deny ... that they had ... that day consumed their soul of the corn, of having behaved with ongentilmensky [ungentlemanly] immodus opposite a pair of dainty maidservants in the swoolth of the rushy hollow...' But the part about the local election comes from Book IV, and the reporters are not soldiers but 'woodwards or regarders', an old term for forest officers protecting venison. (Phoenix Park was noted for its deer.) The soldiers are taken from the page preceding, which states that Earwicker 'lay at one time under the ludicrous imputation of annoying Welsh fusiliers in the people's park' (033.25−7). Never mind the fact that the People's Park is in Dun Laoghaire, nowhere near Phoenix Park.

Now it is clear that **m**, all through FW, is guilty
of something. Often the guilt is connected with
Phoenix Park, oftener with paired girls than indivi-
duals, and **m**'s three enemies are frequently soldiers.
But I could see no utility in the selecting of a particular combination of compatible elements to frame a
'plot'. The same naive realism was evident in Campbell and Robinson's treatment of III.4: 'It is the
morning after the night of the winter solstice. A dry
leaf still clinging to the tree outside the window has
been scratching at the pane; and this sound has drawn
the inexhaustible dream from the depths of the
psyche'[10]. I could see no evidence whatever for this
kind of inference concerning phenomena outside the
sleeper's mind. Campbell and Robinson paint over
everything they don't understand and they are
followed in this by their weaker imitators, such as
Burgess and Tindall.

In contrast to these 'popular' books—ultimately
surrogates for reading FW—a different kind of study
began to appear in the 1950s. I had with me in Paris
Adaline Glasheen's *A Census of Finnegans Wake*
(1956), James Atherton's *The Books at the Wake*
(1959) and Matthew J.C. Hodgart and Mabel P.
Worthington's *Song in the Works of James Joyce*
(1959).[11] The last-named is a fine and accurate
collection of spot-on allusions, but as it says comparatively little about the mechanism of FW, I found
most of my attention focussed on Glasheen and
Atherton.

Both these books continue to uphold the novelistic
approach to a degree. The *Census*, which had two

subsequent editions (1963 and 1977), is an index of persons referred to in FW. The introduction attempts to account for the cast as follows: 'Thousands of people are mentioned in *Finnegans Wake*, but only a handful are characters in the novelist's sense of the word. These characters are the archetypal Earwickers . . . There are five Earwickers—father, mother, twin sons, daughter . . . Archetypes of the second rank include. . . '. etc.[12] There was a table placing a number of personages in columns headed for the five Earwickers but this seemed to me full of inconsistencies, not the least of which was the exclusion of ᚁ.

The novelistic approach assumes that Mr Earwicker's public house in Chapelizod is the factual substrate of FW, which rumours and accidents misrepresent. If you are prepared to read with one eye shut, the viewpoint can be applied to an extent in Book II. Its first chapter shows Earwicker's children playing outside the pub, the second their homework activities within and the third the subsequent drinking scene around closing time. It can be applied in III. 4, where there seems to be some late night activity on the stairs, and in Book IV where the parents are waking up. But in Book I it is hard to defend except in the second chapter, and the same is true of most of Book III.

The Books at the Wake is also novelistic, though aware of the drawbacks of the approach: 'The man lives in Chapelizod with his wife and three children. He is a publican. . . Humpty Dumpty himself, for example, is a symbol of the Fall of Man—he fell off a wall! . . . He is also one facet of H.C.E. He sometimes

seems to be Finnegan.'[13] This is messy thought: all
the persons are simply expressions of ⋔. But Atherton makes up for it with a calm, well-informed
stability that usually brought me into accordance
with his conclusions. The only exceptions were the
occasional claims that Joyce was *attacking* such
persons as Wilde and Carroll (which seemed unduly
kinetic for a godlike artificer), and also the conten-
tion that FW named all the suras of the Koran.

Because I liked Atherton's book more than any of
the others I had with me, I wrote him a letter, care of
his publisher, and learned from the reply that great
things had happened in the world of exegesis. In the
1950s it had been really difficult to publish articles
about FW: editors balked at the ravings of late Joyce.
The nucleus of *Wake* scholarship was the exchange of
letters between Atherton and Hodgart in England and
Glasheen in America. Then, in 1962, Clive Hart and
Fritz Senn founded *A Wake Newslitter*, and a new age
began.

Introducing *A Wake Digest* (1968) Hart describes
the founding of the *Litter*. '*A Wake Newslitter* began
publication in March 1962, having arisen out of conversations between Mr Senn and myself during the
summer of 1961. We planned it as an informal journal
in which studies of *Finnegans Wake* might be quickly
and easily published, so that information about
current Joycean studies could be made readily available to the scholarly fraternity. Its reading public
rapidly increased in numbers so that by February
1964 the *Newslitter* was able to abandon its original
mimeographed format and re-emerge in letterpress.'[14]

The editors at first intended to produce commentaries as 'an extension of something we two have been
doing for some time: telling each other what we
know about *Finnegans Wake*, line by line. . . We
would urge readers who have supplementary information to send it to us. . . Copies of this Newslitter
will be sent free of charge to anyone asking for
them.'[15]   It remained free until it went into letterpress.

In practice, very few sequential analyses of passages appeared, but the editorial to the December
1962 issue makes it clear that public response was
occurring: 'That many of our suggestions are far-
fetched, we agree; some of our correspondents seem
to us to fetch things from a great deal farther; but the
point is to see what needs to be kept, what elimin-
ated, by putting it all together in one place.'[16] Putting it all together was going to become my greatest
problem.

Another stirring event of 1962 was Hart's publication of a book entitled *Structure and Motif in
Finnegans Wake*. This was the first attempt to make a
genuine escape from the novelistic approach. A table
of FW chapters[17], based on Gilbert's well-known
Ulysses schema, gives two columns headed 'PLACE'.
For II.1, one column ('Naturalistic level') reads
'Street in Chapelizod', and the other ('Main narrative
and symbolic levels') reads 'Playhouse'. For II.2 the
respective columns have 'Nursery' and 'Cosmos', for
II.3 'Bar-room' and 'Sevastopol'. Of course this vastly
oversimplifies the issues, but it is encouraging. I was
pleased by Hart's attitude to the *Skeleton Key*:

Tentative, exploratory, and often ill-informed, as its authors were the first to admit, its analyses and judgments have nevertheless been accepted virtually without question by most later critics, with the result that a number of untenable interpretations have been perpetuated year after year.[18]

Hart quoted from Joyce's letters confirming that 'The dream-visions of Book III are a mirror-image of the legends of Book I',[19] but his split of Book I into two halves seemed to me an undesirable *Skeleton Key* heritage. And his view of III.4 as occurring on a separate, lower level of dreaming from the rest of the book seemed threateningly asymmetrical. For me, no change of this nature ought to occur without a balancing event in Book I. I wrote to Hart asking to have the *Newslitter* sent to me, but also voicing my opinion that FW was pivoted around Book II rather than III.4. He replied that his view of FW 'doesn't, as far as I know, centre on any particular part.' I didn't press the point, as I was currently discussing it with Adaline Glasheen. Mrs Glasheen, a housewife in Connecticut, provided extremely prompt and informative replies. Here is a typical Glasheen epistle:

August 6, 1968

Dear Mr McHugh . . . We would all be most grateful to you if you would elucidate crosscorrespondences and/or symbols [sigla]. But you oughtn't to play with symbols until you know precisely what's in the Buffalo notebooks and the ms at the British Museum. I should think a proper study of the symbols would be a very long and often tedious job—years, years—so consider soberly before you leap into it, but indeed I wish you would leap. "I know it is no more than a game but it is a game I have learned to play in my own way. Children may just as well play as not. The ogre will come in any case." [quoting a letter of Joyce in 1926] ... ∧ as answering questions in I.6. Well, between 1st and 2nd censuses I decided Shem asked the questions and Shaun answered. Then came First Draft [Hayman] which seemed to show that Shaun both set questions and answered. Now we've got Letter III 239 which tells us that 126.9 means that the 4 answer the 4th question.???? Speak intelligently to me of this problem. This is a perfect example of what happens when you haven't mastered workbookms material ... I, too, am clear that Book II is balanced by Book IV and Book I by Book III. What does it mean? When we say "balanced by" do we mean opposite ends of a balance? Identity of opposites? Do you think the figure on 293 represents the ideal (if not the exact center) center of FW? It certainly appears with a change of identity for the twins. . . And now I have to go iron clothes and wash walls.

Yrs
A. Glasheen

In Paris there was no easy way of examining all the manuscripts referred to here, so I decided that my best course would be to publish a preliminary statement of my views on FW, and revise it later when I had read the MSS. This I did: 'A Structural Theory of FW' appeared in the December 1968 *Newslitter*, and the eventual result of the revision was a book, *The Sigla of Finnegans Wake*,[20] which came out eight years later. But at the time it was vital that I should somehow pigeonhole structural speculations so as to cope with the astronomical quantity of new data that was coming in.

I began to annotate my copy of FW. I transferred information to it in very small writing, using a mapping pen. I could actually get two lines of writing between every two FW lines, and I used twelve different colours of ink to specify different languages. In addition to the notes I had made in 1965-7 and the sourcebooks I have so far mentioned, there were all the back issues of the *Newslitter* to search through. Then there was the 'Overtones' section of Hart's *A Concordance to Finnegans Wake* (1963).[21] If you look up 'papal' and 'infallibility' in the 'Overtones', both words are assigned to FW 245.12, which gives 'pebble infinibility'. Quite a few of the overtones used in my examples earlier in this book can be found in Hart's index. To acquire the full set it was necessary to look up every page/line reference given, and then write into FW every overtone which I didn't feel was instantly recognizable on the page. It took two months to do this, after which I proceeded to D.B. Christiani's *Scandinavian Elements of Finnegans Wake* (1966), Helmut Bonheim's *A Lexicon of the German in Finnegans Wake* (1967) and Brendan O Hehir's *A Gaelic Lexicon for Finnegans Wake*(1967).[22]

While this was going on I revisited Broughton in England. He told me that my French experience would qualify me for a research assistantship in London to prepare a PhD in grasshopper acoustics. I accordingly withdrew from the French laboratory in November.

Tettigoniid grasshoppers, which were now my concern, are ideal for the student who has other preoccupations. I had to make stereophonic tape recordings of pairs of males singing to one another, and as they do this only during the late summer and early autumn one is not overworked during the remainder of the year. Grasshopper sexuality is primarily acoustic: a female will walk away from a silent male towards a loudspeaker emitting male song. So each male surrounds itself with a fluid territory which it keeps saturated with its own song. I eventually discovered that professors at James Joyce Symposia behaved similarly.

I first heard about the Symposia from the other *Newslitter* editor, Fritz Senn. There existed, it appeared, a James Joyce Foundation in Tulsa, Oklahoma, and they had held a first Symposium in Dublin in June 1967. Senn was now organizing the second, due also to take place in Dublin, in June 1969. Both Hart and himself would be there, and I agreed to join a discussion group on 'The Issy Figure'. I decided to make the point that in a letter of 1924 Joyce designates Issy ⊥, but that in another of 1926 there are several Issy sigla, ⊣ , ⊥ and ⊢ . From the few manuscript sigla I had at my disposal it appeared that some change of conceptualisation had occurred between those dates. I was hopeful that some member of the audience would contribute constructively to my speculations, perhaps from a better acquaintance with the manuscripts.

On the day before the Symposium opened I was walking the Dublin streets in the very agreeable company of Mr Hart and Mr Senn. Clive Hart, an Australian of a jovial and tolerant disposition, was like myself trained in the sciences—physics in fact—and was also a major international authority on medieval kites and windsocks. Fritz Senn of Zurich combined   a sort of religious anxiety about the week's coming 'hostilities' with the characteristic indifference of anyone who has spent over a decade trying to focus the cosmic joke.

I was slightly daunted at being accepted this readily by people who knew so much more than I about Joycean activities. We walked along the route taken by Lenehan and McCoy in 'The Wandering Rocks', and landmarks from that episode were casually mentioned as we passed them. As a biologist I had a long-established respect for field research—in fact as soon as the Symposium finished I was to fly to the South of France and join Broughton who was collecting grasshoppers there. I perceived that in visiting Dublin four years earlier I had barely touched the contours of the labyrinth.

The Symposium itself was safely ensconced behind the walls of Trinity College. In its distance from reality it resembled the district attorneys' conference in *Fear and Loathing in Las Vegas*. As I sat listening to American professors reading papers which paraphrased the plots of the stories in *Dubliners* or compared *Ulysses* with the novels of Faulkner I sensed a kind of gap. Virtually no-one present was Irish, so I was unlikely to learn anything about local colour. And as far as the *Newslitter* went, most of them had barely heard of it. They read something called *James Joyce Quarterly*, a glossy production from Oklahoma, largely devoted to the early Joyce industry.[23]

When the Issy panel came up I drew sigla all over the blackboard and looked at the audience. No response. Egyptian hieroglyphics would have done just as well. An argument began over the word 'Tip', which occurs repeatedly in FW 8-9; did it mean the tip of the penis? I could smell ignorance of the text. Most of the people hadn't read FW any further than those pages, and lacking any precise information they tended to fall back on the obscene allusion as a panacea.

It was impossible to get down to intelligent discussion of FW at any point during the week. People shied off, as though talking shop were bad form. Much of the conversation I overheard was of the order 'Say! How much dough do you make?' Hart had to return to England at an early stage with the guest of honour, Frank Budgen, and Senn was far too busy organizing events to discuss theory. As he wrote to me later 'for quiet intense talks the Symposium was not the proper atmosphere'.

There were of course other *Newslitter* contributors present, but the only ones with whom I talked at any length were Jack Dalton (see below, pp.71-77), and the leading Dutch Joycean, Leo Knuth. A lecturer in Old English, Knuth had a thorough acquaintance with etymology and linguistics, which made his digressions on any item in FW a source of fascination for me. He would also quote Shakespeare at great length from memory, for example with a pullover rammed up his jacket to represent Richard III's hump. I told him that I was thinking of writing a lexicon of obscure English in FW, and later that year I sent him a manuscript, to which he added generously. But it was never resolved into a separate book, and eventually joined

the other tiny notes scribbled between the lines of
my FW.

In November a Dutch translation of *Ulysses* was
published, and Knuth invited me to Holland for the
celebrations. Both *Newslitter* editors were there, and
once the book was launched we found ourselves, with
a few other enthusiasts, in a Mr de Leeuw's house in
Haarlem. A discussion began on the desirability of
private meetings at which detailed analyses of FW
could be conducted. This was the birth of the 'European *Finnegans Wake* Study Group', the name
suggested to me by the British Spider Study Group.
During the subsequent two years, the Group examined in close detail the opening of the dialogue between 'Butt' and 'Taff' in II.3. We felt that if we were
going to make this much effort, we might as well
examine a really difficult passage. Beginning in
Amsterdam in April 1970, we worked our way from
338.04 to 339.30. In October we moved thence to
340.30, also in Amsterdam. In April 1971 we held a
meeting in Brighton, which James Atherton attended,
and reached 342.32, where we paused to reconsider
our purposes.

The first meeting was probably the best. About
fourteen persons sat comfortably in armchairs in
Gerry Franken's large front room. Matthew Hodgart
acted as chairman. A tape recorder in the centre of
the room was kept running and we had a collection of
reference books at hand. Of course, FW 338 had
already been scrutinized in the early *Newslitter*. Here
is an extract from Taff's second speech, followed by
the appropriate *Newslitter* gloss, and then our discussion of it:

Sling Stranaslang, how Malorazzias spikes her, coining a
speak a spake! Not the Setanik stuff that slimed soft
Siranouche! The good old gunshop monowards for
manosymples. Tincurs tammit! They did oak hay doe
fou Chang-li-meng when that man d'airain was big top
tom saw tip side bum boss pageantfiller. (338.22-7)

This was glossed as follows in the September 1962
Newslitter:

338.22 Sling Stranaslang - slang and strange (It., strano)
languages; strana (Rus.) = region, area; Saint
Stanislaus (?)
Malorazzias - malorusskii (Ukraine dial.); razzia
(Iy.) = raid, insect-powder; malora (It.) = ruin
338.23 spikes her - speaks it
coining a speak a spake - calling a spade a spade;
putting the present into the past (why?); coining a
phrase
Setanik - Satanic; Nick; Set, the Satanic brother of
Osiris; sotnik (Rus.) = captain of a sotnia (= a
group of — originally 100 — soldiers); seta (It.) =
silk, stuff
338.24 Siranouche - Cyrano + Scaramouche; Sir Anush -
Anush was a Hittite god of the heavens; in the
Mandaean sect the true Christ is named Anush, so
that we may have here a true and a false Christ
gunshop monowards - ship; man-o'-war; ginshop
(pub)
338.25 manosymples - man of samples; simples; manciples;
symbols
Tincurs tammit - tinker's dam [*sic*]; tincture
They did oak hay doe fou - Golden Bough theme;
O.K.; fou (Fr.) = mad (Bacchic madness)
338.26 Chang-li-meng - Charlemagne; change + mengen
(Ger.) = mix
man d'airain - man of brass; man of Erin; man of
Aran; man of iron; daring man (in circus—see

below); mandarin; air and rain; Air, in Phoenician
Creation legend; Air and Chaos were in the beginning; Aryan

big top - circus tent (all kinds of public spectacle
are involved in 'Butt and Taff')

top tom saw - topsawyer (3.07)

top tom ... tip - Tom Tit Tot (the folk-tale);
(260.02)

saw tip - saw-pit

tip side bum boss - (quasi-pidgin) HCE is god; bum
boss-homosexuality; pimple on HCE's backside
564.28   ; bumbo = drink made from rum, sugar,
water and nutmeg; tip side - HCE pours drinks; joss
= God; (611.27)

338.27 Bambus (Ger.) = bamboo

pageantfiller - pageant feller; filler of glasses; ant
(?); pa + géant (Fr.) = giant + fille (Fr.) = daughter
(HCE in his typical incestuous role)[24]

Now the discussion:

Matthew Hodgart: Sling, sing. Apart from 'Sing slang',
strana, a country.

A woman's voice: A town.

Hodgart: A town. In Russian a country.

Woman's voice: A region.

Hodgart: Ah, a region, not a country. *Slang*, a snake
[Dutch]. Malorazzias, mala. Ukrainian.

Rosa Maria Bosinelli: A curse in Italian.

Hodgart: It's a curse. How d'you spell it?

Bosinelli: MALARAZZA. It also means a mandrake.

Hodgart: And the corresponding thing in Russian,
how's it spelled? The Ukrainian.

Roland McHugh: MALORUSSKII. You've got -KII in
the *Litter* and -KIJ in your Russian list.

Leo Knuth: Malora?

Hodgart: Sounds Russian.

Clive Hart: Capital M: who is intended?

Hodgart: The Devil. Old Satan himself. Pun on 'snake'.

Bosinelli: It might be the Italian.

McHugh: I'll see what Glasheen says.

Hodgart: This reminds me of P.W Joyce's *English as we Speak it in Ireland*, which is a very important source.

Fritz Senn: Also *English as She is Spoke.*

Hodgart: There might be a sexual level too. Helen might be Eve and this might be referring to the legend that the Serpent had sexual relations with Eve.

Knuth: Now, the snake or the Devil, apparently a *strange* creature, huh? Strana. And what about the sling? Sling Slang. Strange languages? The slings and arrows of outrageous fortune?

Hodgart: Yes, great. *Hamlet*, sure. Also King David's sling. Now, 'calling a spade a spade'.

Hart: And the implied opposite: coining an expression.

Hodgart: That's right.

Knuth: And perhaps the coil of the snake.

Hodgart: Coil.

Hart: Stranaslang sounds like Stanislaus.

A voice: Does, doesn't it? Stanislaus.

Knuth: Why's speak spake? I mean the present tense. Here we find ablaut in the original linguistic sense, huh?

Hodgart: Perhaps he means the Indo-European ablaut

in the language spoken by Eve and the snake.

Bosinelli: Or Joyce's opinion of the Italians he had to teach English. They pronounced words as they were written, so 'speak' would sound like 'spake'.

[laughter]

Hodgart: 'Siranouche' means 'love-sweet' in Armenian.

McHugh: Appearing just like that in the notebook.[25]

Hodgart: The thing about the notebook is it's all taken down in French spelling. French Armenian.

Hart: Slimed soft love-sweet?? What does that mean?

Hodgart: A term of endearment maybe? Little Eve?

Knuth: This is interesting: we find Satan, we find the centurion Panther, Christ's father, in the Russian word for a centurion, *sotnik,* and we find Christ himself in Anush. The Mandaean sect called Christ Anush.

Hodgart: What about Scaramouche?

Knuth: Originally Scaramouche is a buffoon, of course, *Scaramuccia*. He gets beaten every time by a harlequin.

G.J.H. de Leeuw: And Cyrano.

Knuth: Yes, Cyrano in French. I don't think so.

Hart: He was not notably soft.

Hodgart: So it seems to say 'let's have no more of this soft talk by which the snake seduced Eve and the centurion Mary.'

de Leeuw: And seduction practiced by soldiers in the Crimean War.

Knuth: There's an Italian word *seta.* Italian *seta* means silk, doesn't it?

Bosinelli: Yes.

Knuth: Set, the satanic brother of Osiris.

Hodgart: A lot of what's come up in the last few minutes has been relèvant in a way.

Knuth: Nick of course is another word for the Devil.

Hodgart: The good old gunshop monowards for manosymples. In Grose's dictionary [which Joyce possessed], when you get four-letter words he uses 'monosyllable'.

de Leeuw: Mono-words for many symbols.

Hodgart: Could be the gunship coming up to Liberty Hall. [338.20 'leporty hole']

Knuth: Shelling Liberty Hall. [During the Easter Rising in Dublin.]

Hodgart: The Royal Military Academy in England at Woolwich was known as 'the Shop'. Not the gunshop, just the shop.

Knuth: Man-o'-war of course too. Manoeuvres?

Bosinelli: Move onwards?

Hodgart: 'Half a league, half a league, half a league onward!'

Senn: The aim of the Light Brigade was to retrieve the guns, the cannons, eh?

Bosinelli: *Mano* means a hand in Italian.

Hodgart: The man of war and the man of samples. Then there's a tinker's curse or tinker's damn it. Finnish word is *tammi*, oak. Means an oak.

Knuth: But I don't see what the oak. . .

Hodgart: I don't see either, but as the Finnish word is there in translation it must be right.

McHugh: Yes. It's funny, that. *Tammi* means oak.

Hodgart: This is a very hard bit now. Oak hay. O.K.

Senn: Now we get the words of one syllable, mm?

Chinese?

Hodgart: Oak hay fou. O.K. do fou.

McHugh: Okey doke.

Knuth: *Auto-da-fé.*

de Leeuw: The oak again: it's phallic. You have the oak and then after three words you have fou. Hay hi and fu, Chinese. Yung hi, a Chinese dish.

Knuth: Is there Chinese here? French *fou*?

McHugh: I don't think much if this is Chinese.

Hodgart: Man d'airain. Mandarin. Anyone remember a Chinese Charlemagne? And French *airain*, brass. Man of brass, man of Erin, man of iron. . .

Chorus of Voices: The Iron Duke.

Hodgart: Wellington. Airain, air and rain, two elements. Big top tom saw tip side bum boss. Big top: the big top in the circus. Tom saw: *Tom Sawyer*. In pidgin English topside usually means above.

de Leeuw: Page-filler. Top side: he is mounting.

McHugh: Curious the word's applied to the General here and to Buckley at 611, line 4: 'topside joss pidgin fella Balkelly'.

de Leeuw: Charlemagne was a pagan-killer.

Hodgart: Pagan-killer, yes. I wonder does it mean that literally? That Charlemagne was top side pagan-killer. But then what does the earlier part of the sentence mean: 'oak hay doe fou'?

de Leeuw: *Auto-da-fé,* O.K.

Hodgart: Of course! Burning pagans and heretics. *Bosse* of course is also 'hump'. Of course pageant filler, I mean, the first part is also *géant*, hm? Giant.

Knuth: Giant-killer.

Hodgart: Jack the Giant-Killer.

Some of the participants said virtually nothing, and one wondered how much of it they were missing. At an early stage Matthew Hodgart underlined a distinction: the maximizers, such as himself, were delighted at every additional level that could be envisaged ('Yes, great. *Hamlet,* sure. Also King David's sling.'). On the other hand minimizers such as myself tried to cut the allusions to the smallest number which would account for all the letters in the word. The sessions were characterized by alternations of long silences with excited spasms when everybody talked at once.

Possibly because I was analysing grasshopper recordings at the time I opted to transcribe the tapes of the sessions. This enabled me to reflect on the proceedings. Was this really the best way to explore FW? Some of the statements are untrustworthy. For example I was nowhere able to confirm Mrs Bosinelli's *malarazza*. And can one assume that because Scaramouche is approved by Hodgart and Knuth, and Cyrano rejected by Hart and Knuth, that the former is acceptable to the masses and the latter not? It began eventually to seem as though the cost of housing a multinational study group, collecting them from the airport and so on, was not entirely justified by the results. We depended on the hospitality of de Leeuw, Hodgart and Mrs Franken, having no kind of grant or connection with an official body.

Consequently, we planned no further meetings after that in April 1971, but there was to be another International Symposium in June, this time in Trieste. I converted the transcriptions into a lecture. Here, as

an illustration, is what became of the passage just
considered, as subsequently published in the *Atti del
Third International James Joyce Symposium:*

> Use countrified slang: Malorusskii, the Ukraine dialect,
> calling a spade a spade and coining new forms of speech.
> Let's have no more of this soft talk by which the Snake
> seduced Eve and the Centurion Mary, (I'll also explain
> that later). The good old monosyllabic words for many
> symbols, damm [*sic*; the *Atti* crawl with misprints] it.
> They did okey doke (*tammi* is Finnish for oak), they did
> okey doke for Charlemagne, when that mandarin, man
> of brass, man of iron, Iron Duke, Wellington, was on top
> as pagan killer and *géant* killer, giantkiller. . . . Continu-
> ing with the Russian . . . Malorisskij [*sic*] is the Ukraine
> dialect. In the succeeding line a *Sotnik* is the captain of a
> *Sotnia*, a group of – originally – 100 soldiers. This
> suggested to us Panther, the Roman centurion who
> according to a legend was Christ's real father. We also
> find Christ himself in 'Siranouche' – the name Anush
> was used for Christ by the Mandaean sect, and 'Siran-
> ouche' resembles the Armenian word meaning 'love-
> sweet'. There is manuscript evidence that Joyce intended
> the word to be Armenian. Further, *slang,* in 'Stranas-
> lang' is Dutch for 'snake', so we have Christ, the Devil
> and the Centurion. It was this which led us to read the
> sentence: 'Let's have no more of this soft talk by which
> the Snake seduced Eve and the Centurion Mary'. *Strana*
> is Russian for 'country'. Countrified slang. . . . Of course
> *topside* is Chinese Pidgin for 'above' and the phrase
> echoes page 611, line 4: 'topside joss pidgin fella Bal-
> kelly'. 'Pageantfiller' also seems to resemble 'pagan
> killer'. They did O.K. for Charlemagne when that man
> was pagankiller. Well, he certainly killed pagans, so
> perhaps the earlier part of the sentence 'oak hay doe
> fou' could suggest *auto-da-fé*, which would be appro-
> priate to pagan killing. [26]

One morning at the Symposium I read out this lecture. The audience had copies of the FW passage (338.04-341.17) to follow it with and the whole thing went on for an hour. There were no questions from the floor. The quality of scholarship was noticeably down on last time, although the treatment given us by the Triestines was magnificent. I treated the occasion as an excuse to see another of Joyce's cities. It is strange to contemplate pages which evoke the damp Dublin streets as having been written in the glare of the Adriatic coast. But it was the end of my involvement with Joyce Symposia and I have never been to another.

As my PhD neared completion during the late summer of 1971 I began to feel a distaste for life in large cities, particularly London. Clive Hart was at this time Professor of English at Dundee University. I suggested to him, during an abortive FW Study Group session at Aachen, that I would like to move to Scotland. I added that, as he and I seemed to have between us an extremely large mass of FW glosses, I would like to extract from it a single typescript, containing all the good material in as compact a form as possible. This project eventually became *Annotations to Finnegans Wake*. Hart was agreeable, although he could not, unfortunately, offer me a job in Dundee. I decided to go anyway. I loaded my possessions into my car and drove out on to the A1 motorway. Somewhere between Newcastle and Jedburgh the country began to look wilder and I started to feel better. I continued full of optimism.

4
The British Museum manuscripts

Joyce's composition of FW occupied seventeen years, during which time he had few other occupations. He also, of course, spent a good deal of time lying down in darkened rooms, recovering from eye operations, and his poor vision helped to obscure his calligraphy. Thus one of the qualifications required of the manuscript scholar is the ability to decipher a jumble of cramped and distorted lettering.

For every chapter of the *Wake* there are a succession of *witnesses*, as they are called: drafts, typescripts, proofs and printed versions. Most of them are embellished with numerous additions and corrections in the author's hand. Joyce gave nearly all of this material to his patron, Miss Weaver, who later donated it to the British Museum. It is bound there in a collection of large volumes numbered B.M. Additional MSS 47471-47488.

The manuscripts spread their shadow slowly over the pathways of FW exegesis. Matthew Hodgart had a look at them in the 1950s and noticed, for example, that the rather similar III.1 and III.2 were originally constructed as a single chapter. In 1960

Clive Hart published a paper[1] noting certain disparities between the printed FW and the earlier versions, but this was ahead of its time and made little impact on pre-*Newslitter* society. The next phase was a controversy concerning Kiswahili. One Philipp Wolff, who had lived in Africa, recognized a number of words in FW as belonging to that language. He sent a list to Campbell, the *Skeleton Key* co-author, but received no acknowledgement. Then, hearing of the *Newslitter,* he passed the list to Fritz Senn and it appeared in the December 1962 issue.[2]

Some of the words were undeniably correct. For instance at 199.19-20 Anna Livia offers m a ham sandwich (German, *Schinkenbrot,* made with French *jambon*, ham): 'a shinkobread (hamjambo, bana?) for to plaise that man'. Wolff noticed the Kiswahili greeting *Hajambo, bwana*? At 200.33 'And what was the wyerye rima she made!' means 'And what was the weary rhyme (Italian, *rima*) she made?', plus the rivers Wye and Rima (the fluidity of I.8 is enhanced by the inclusion of over a thousand river-names). Here Wolff saw Kiswahili *rima,* 'pit for catching large animals'. Obviously a less useful gloss, but how can you presume to say that Kiswahili *rima* is 'wrong'? A paper by Jack P. Dalton in the April 1963 *Litter* provided the answer. You do it with the manuscripts:

> I am not so much interested in Kisuahili, or in Herr Wolff's performance, or the Litter's performance, as I am concerned with the foundation of logical principles and practices on which FW scholarship must come to rest, if it is ever to amount to anything more than a stumbling block to the serious student, and a butt of

derision for scoffers. . . Now the list I have presented [a
modification of Wolff's] . . . stands quite perfectly on its
own two feet, as it were. However, there is a most interesting aspect of it not yet noted—*all the words in the list
. . . were added to FW at the same time.* I refer to the
second galleys for the FW ALP, B.M. Add. MS 47476A.
261-275. . . There remain to note, then, the seven cita-
tions which I have completely dropped from Herr
Wolff's list. . . The items . . . were added . . . all 10 years
or so prior. . . These items haven't a leg to stand on anyway, but the loss of context cuts the ground from under
them as well.[3]

In other words, if a number of items were all added
to a particular witness of a FW chapter, they bolster
one another in their chances of deriving from a speci-
fied source. Material like this tends to be clustered in
small areas of text, so proximity to the main nucleus
further increases the likelihood of relevance.

Of course the exigencies of reading FW leave few
readers with the energy to check their findings against
the MSS. There is also the problem of access. Until
recently, if one did not live in London, it was necessary to purchase microfilm of the B.M. collection
(and also, naturally, to have a microfilm reader at
hand). But in 1977 publication began of a set of
facsimiles, as part of a general edition of Joyce's
manuscripts, *The James Joyce Archive.*[4] The witnesses we are discussing take up twenty of the sixty-
three *Archive* volumes, and are accompanied by a
chronological analysis of the growth of each chapter,
by Danis Rose, who also arranged the pages into a
more coherent sequence than Miss Weaver's. The
availability of the *Archive* will add considerable

momentum to *Wake* studies: even Dublin now has a couple of sets, in the National Library and Trinity College.

We live in privileged times. When Dalton's paper on the Kiswahili appeared it must have seemed that the right of the layman to present his guesswork in the genial forum of the *Litter* was threatened. The next issue carried a rebuff from Clive Hart:

> It is certainly possible, by means of a reversal of Joyce's process of composition, to extract and isolate the deposits of discrete pieces of denotation from which the book was originally compounded. I am not suggesting that this pursuit will lead to a denial of the interrelationships of constituent parts, nor that it claims the whole to be no more than the sum of its parts. What I am suggesting, however, is that it is a major example of a most restrictive fallacious intentionalism.[5]

Looming behind all the practicalities of FW research in the 1960s was the great schism between Dalton's Intentionalism and Hart's Anti-intentionalism. To the reader daunted by the volume of the MSS, the Anti-intentionalist approach has an obvious appeal, and as Hart says, it 'seems, paradoxically, to have Joyce's sanction—to have been, as it were, part of his intention'.[6] For instance in the letter we quoted earlier, where 'violer' is glossed 'viola in all moods and senses'.[7] Hart wrote to me in 1968: 'Most modern critics will say, rightly or wrongly, that it doesn't matter a damn what any author intended, except in so far as that intention is borne out by the work itself. "For all we know, JJ may have intended FW to be a cookery book. Who cares what he thought? What are the *book's* intentions?" '.

Now, this argument is theoretically unanswerable.
But for most readers, a satisfied conviction that a
particular interpretation is apt will rarely occur without at least a suspicion of authorial intent. And Anti-
intentionalism is a fearful stimulus to what is known
as the 'lunatic fringe' of FW studies. As Hart himself
observes of the *Wake*, 'Too often its convolutions
have been treated as a kind of endless verbal equi-
valent of the Rorschach Ink-blot Test.'[8] Against this
backdrop, the restrictive quality of the manuscript
approach seems a welcome curb. Instead of the un-
committed impartiality of the maximizer we see the
jesuitical precision of the dealer in probabilities. The
typical manuscript scholar is obsessed by the need for
precision. A good example can be seen in Dalton's 'I
Say It's Spinach – "Watch!" ', which took up the
whole of the November 1963 *Litter*. This is a review
of David Hayman's *A First Draft Version of Finnegans Wake.*[9] Hayman had attempted to transcribe the
earliest drafts of each FW chapter, but Dalton showed
so many transcription errors in his work that its
utility as a whole became questionable. The tone of
his review—slow, nit-picking evisceration inter-
spersed with clouds of vitriolic indignation and cheap
sarcasm—has helped to create an image of the FW
exegete as a man for whom worldly issues retreat
before the conflicts of commas and semicolons.
'Damn it, Hayman, you make me ill with rage. The
creation of such monstrous vile filth as this, and all
the rest of it, should be a criminal offense, necessarily
capital. That it is not is a grave defect of our
society.'[10]

This is all harmless comedy, but as Dalton edged forwards his pronouncements became more disconcerting. I think everyone interested in textual problems ought to read his 'Advertisement for the Restoration', which appeared in 1966 in a collection edited by Hart and himself, *Twelve and a Tilly.*

The article considers one of the most transparent portions of FW, the meditation of St Kevin (605.04-606.12). Various ecclesiastical and celestial hierarchies are dotted across it. Here is a dissected version, displaying one of them, the nine orders of angels. I have italicized the orders to facilitate recognition:

> Procreated ... come their feast of precreated holy whiteclad *angels* ... Kevin ... came ... to our own midmost Glendalough-le-vert by *archangel*ical guidance ... whereof its lake is the ventrifugal *principality*, whereon by prime, *power*ful in knowledge, Kevin ... acolyte of cardinal *virtues* ... carrying that privileged altar ... ninthly en*throned* ... his *cherub*ical loins ... he meditated continuously with *seraph*ic ardour the primal sacrament of baptism or the regeneration of all man by affusion of water.

Pious readers will immediately remark the absence of one order, dominations, which ought to come between virtues and thrones. Dalton isn't pious, but he noticed it too, and went to the manuscripts. Looking at an early draft he found in place of 'carrying that privileged altar' an additional line of writing, making it 'carrying the lustral domination contained within his most portable privileged altar'. He concluded that 'mindful of the cardinal fact that *exactly one line* was excised, even the most sober attempts at justification seem to me sophistical in the extreme. In fact, it must be considered that the primary effect of omitting the line was not to leave out an order of angels, but to wreck the syntax of the sentence.'[11]

Having demonstrated the existence of what might be described as an *error* in FW, Dalton went on to demonstrate more, and stated that he knew of over six hundred, adding however that 'not every one, of course, is as choice as these'. The solution he proposed was an emendation of the text. It is at this station that I cease to concur with his viewpoint.

Textual emendation is an issue relevant to other texts besides FW, for example *Ulysses*. At Munich, Hans Walter Gabler is currently directing the production of a critical edition, consisting of two parts. The 'synoptic text', on the left-hand pages, uses numbered half-brackets to label the stages of accretion and full brackets to label deleted items. Removal of the brackets and deletions gives the 'critical plain text', to be carried by the right-hand pages. Publication is expected around 1983, according to Hugh Kenner.[12]

I will certainly buy Gabler's book and use it in place of the currently available *Ulysses*. There are bound to be a few erroneous changes, but by and large we understand the meaning of the novel. FW, however, is different. It can sometimes appear to be unreasonable nonsense whilst remaining utterly coherent for the reader who holds the key. And we never know what additional level of meaning might be lying dormant, waiting to shed illumination over some tract which looks fully explicated but isn't. In such cases what looks like a misprint might be a vital link in the new reading. Certainly, the line with 'domination' seems to have been omitted by Joyce's oversight, and its omission appears to be entirely reductive in impact, but it is in fact the thin end of the wedge. Admit it an error and a forest of new errors begin to clamour for attention.

Dalton believes, according to his article, that 'Siker of calmy days' (237.31) should be changed to read 'Siku of calmy days'. The word *siku* is Kiswahili for 'day', and we can certainly demonstrate that Joyce appreciated this when he inserted the item into the text. But what exactly did he insert? Dalton says 'Siku': 'The "u" Joyce wrote was sloppy, with suggestions of loops in the minims; the first was read as "e", the second followed as "r"'.[13] I would maintain that the mark cannot be definitively judged a 'u' or an 'er': it is something between the two. But if we retain 'Siker' in the text I can still accept Kiswahili *siku* as an overtone in it. Change it to 'Siku' and you destroy the English overtone 'seeker', producing a less beautiful sentence which means solely 'day of calm/balmy days'. Being part of a speech addressed to a person, is it not more reasonable that he should be called a seeker than a day?

To appreciate the situation in relation to the progression of witnesses, we might look at the erosion which has affected 124.09-12. In his early paper on the text, Hart says 'This typographical carnival has suffered more corruption than any other single passage in *Finnegans Wake*'.[14] Before we look at it, a word about its rationale might be in order.

I.5, as explained earlier, is an account of the letter (◻), working towards the determination of its authorship. As one of the ingredients in ◻ is *The Book of Kells*, which was dated by an analysis of its punctuation,[15] the punctuation marks of ◻ become significant at the end of I.5, and are said to have been 'provoked' by the fork of a professor, to introduce a notion of time. Because, as Samuel Beckett said, FW 'is not *about* something; *it is that something itself*',[16] it is appropriate that a mass of distinctive punctuation should appear at just this point in the text. This explains one piece of insanity, the double semicolon (;;), but to augment the effect Joyce sprinkled diacritics over the region indicated. As these differ in the different witnesses one might claim that dating by punctuation, as with *The Book of Kells*, can actually apply to the FW text itself.

We will examine only a fragment of the sentence. Part of the first draft, probably written around 26 February 1925, says of the marks that

they ăd bin "provòked" by ∧ fork,
ŏf á grave Profès̄s̸or

Joyce's typist copied this fairly well, including the stroke through the second 's' in 'Professor', but making the marks above both 'of' and 'a' resemble slightly curved grave accents. Later the passage was retyped, and they were straightened in the process, becoming identical with the grave accent in 'Professor'. At the same time the second 's' was removed, the stroke being presumably taken as a deletion mark, although Joyce does not normally delete in this fashion.

Next, the chapter was printed in the July 1925 number of T.S. Eliot's magazine *The Criterion*, and two new changes appeared: the second word was now 'ăd', and 'by' had become 'ay'. On *Criterion* pages prepared for the printer of another magazine, *transition*, Joyce changed the 'P' of 'Professor' to a 'B', but in the proofs they returned him they had not only complied with this request, but also removed the accent from its remaining 's', and those from 'ad', 'of' and 'provoked'. These alterations being retained in the August 1926 *transition*, it was left to the Faber and Faber printer to remove the mark over 'they' in 1937, and the words arrived at their present state.

Is it safe to assume that all those changes were accidents? Joyce did, after all, restore on all three sets of Faber galleys the grave accent five words further on, in 'professionally', presumably by reference to a copy of *transition*. Hart's paper notes 'the change to "ay" was probably intentional', but if so, why not also the change in 'ad' in *The Criterion*, which restores a type of accent used in the first draft, although on a different word? Ask somebody else and you'll get a third opinion. No two manuscript specialists can ever be expected to agree on what ought, and what ought not, to be altered. The conception of a 100% accurate text of FW strikes me as a dangerously idealistic abstraction.

Let's go back to 'Siker of calmy days'. Emendation of this phrase would be reductive: clarification of one level whilst another is obliterated. Nearly everything in FW means several different things at once, and the danger of the manuscript approach is

that its proponents often fall prey to single-narrative
readings, the narrative that the MS happens to account for. I suspect that Joyce would frequently
observe some secondary interpretation or enrichment
resulting from the ambiguity of a misprint. Although
the effect might be to damage the syntax or coher-
ence of the primary level, he might well opt for
leaving it, such was his greed for multiplicity of meanings. Who are we to challenge such decisions?

In 1967, Peter du Sautoy, the vice-chairman of
Faber and Faber, concluded in the *Newslitter* that a
variorum edition might be 'the only way out, but I do
not see it at the moment as something either feasible
or economic for FW.'[17] I'm inclined to agree that it's
the only way out. But the first requirement is that
the text be fully investigated, and Dalton's attention
seems now to have swerved away to *Ulysses*. (He long
ago submitted a '90% correct' version to Random
House, which I hope they won't just sit on.) Most of
the recent textual commentary has come from Danis
Rose and Ian MacArthur.

At present Rose is apparently constructing a
synoptic version of FW on the same lines as Gabler's
Ulysses. This ought to provoke some disagreement
when it appears, and the final aim, of course, is to
replace the edition commonly found on bookshelves
with a critical plain text extracted in the same
manner as with *Ulysses*. I think it unfortunate that
one set of decisions should simply be adopted in
bulk as the right answer, but of course a study of
Rose's text ought to show up most of the apparent
misprints (he claims there are about four thousand),

and if these are then properly documented by checking against the MSS it should not be too difficult to convert the list into footnotes for a variorum edition.

In spite of his earlier committment to pure Daltonism in the *Litter*,[18] Ian MacArthur tells me he now agrees that a variorum edition is the best solution. MacArthur is a chemist in Norwich, and has published various 'textual studies' of parts of the *Wake*.[19] I particularly liked his piece on the 'F sigla', laterally inverted pairs of capital Fs which occur at a few points in FW. In some cases the printed letters are not precisely inverted. MacArthur observes 'From the various emendations that Joyce made, it appears that an essential feature of the motif is that the letters should be mirror images. Note, for example, 18.36, where the original pair was altered to enantiomorphs in draft [6]. The Fs at 121.03,07 underwent a rotation as Joyce altered the surviving original to mirror the corruption. The passage at 468.03 confirms this, where the Fs are directly linked to the pq motif.'[20]

When we are dealing with issues as complex as this it is not enough for the manuscript expert merely to point out the stages at which a word or letter changed: he has to argue, to explain why the changes occurred. What I should like to see is not a synoptic version of FW but rather a thorough analytical discussion of possible textual abberations, preferably with photographs of particularly uncertain items in the handwriting. The footnotes in a variorum edition would be keyed to this volume for rapid reference, and would therefore be fairly compact in themselves, and not get in the reader's way. We just need somebody to do it.

5
The Buffalo notebooks

The original blurb sent out by the editors of *The James Joyce Archive* describes the twenty volumes of witnesses we considered in the last chapter. It also lists sixteen volumes of facsimiles of *Finnegans Wake* notebooks, which, it says, 'constitute the dark continent of *Wake* studies'. It will be remembered that Adaline Glasheen advised me in 1968 to find out 'precisely what's in the Buffalo notebooks' before venturing to explain sigla. This was, of course, long before the *Archive* was published. When I moved to London I found it easy to call at the British Museum for the material there, but the notebooks could not be purchased even on microfilm. The State University of New York at Buffalo, owners of the material, were prepared to loan microfilms in twos, but this made the examination of the entire collection a slow and awkward business. I began studying the notebooks in the autumn of 1969, and found, like the French Joycean Jacques Aubert, that the complete process took about two years.

The Buffalo notebooks were never donated to Miss Weaver. Joyce kept them in his Paris flat, perhaps uncertain as to whether or not they merited preservation. Possibly he thought he might need them to remind him of the meaning of parts of his book. Possibly he contemplated using them in a subsequent work. Possibly he was waiting to see how FW exegesis would progress before deciding whether or not to destroy them. When he moved out of Paris during the Nazi occupation he left them behind, conceivably feeling he had done well to let chance determine their survival. The notebooks outlasted the war; Joyce didn't.

Buffalo acquired the material in 1950 and eventually published a catalogue giving a breakdown of the contents.[1] There are sixty-six notebooks numbered as follows:

VI.A	One large notebook in Joyce's hand.
VI.B.1-40; 42-8	Forty-seven small notebooks in Joyce's hand, the last being post-FW and therefore un-important.
VI.C.1-18	Eighteen notebooks contain-ing copies by Mme France Raphael of most of the 'B' notebooks.
VI.B.41	A quantity of notes in Joyce's hand at the end of VI.C.18.
VI.Đ.1-7	Parts of VI.C.1-18: Mme Raphael's copies of notebooks whose originals have dis-appeared.

The copying of material into the 'C' series was necessitated by the condition of Joyce's eyesight, which made it difficult for him to read his own hand-writing. Mme Raphael made a good many transcriptions but inevitably produced errors as she knew so little about his work. As Dalton showed,[2] some of those errors eventually got into FW, adding an extra touch of chaos to the emendation dilemma.

Notebook VI.A is not one of the most interesting, but it may have been its size which persuaded Thomas E. Connolly to transcribe and publish a version of it in 1961 under the title *Scribbledehobble,* which is the first word of its text.[3] *Scribbledehobble* is notoriously inaccurate: a list of corrigenda published by David Hayman[4] is only part of the story.

VI.B.1-48 have been treated more professionally: extracts and analyses have appeared in the *Newslitter*, and one complete notebook, VI.B.46, has been published as an edited transcription with copious notes. This is Danis Rose's *The Index Manuscript*.[5] I suppose one could say that a good many of the earlier notebooks read something like *Scribbledehobble* and that the later ones increasingly resemble *The Index Manuscript*. There is still a frightful amount of work to be done.

We can divide the contents of the Buffalo notebooks into five categories:

1. Isolated scraps of information, often cryptically abbreviated.
2. Lists, either of words in a particular language or of extracts from a particular sourcebook.
3. Phrases which are also found, sometimes in a modified form, in the FW text itself. Occasionally these are extended to become short

sections of first-draft material; sometimes a whole paragraph of FW will occur in its earliest form in some notebook.

4. Sigla entries and other statements relating to the internal structuring of FW.

5. Personalia, addresses, phone numbers and general rubbish.

Let's begin with an example of the first category. In a letter of March 1931 Joyce informed Miss Weaver of his efforts to compose II.1, 'trying to follow with various readers the books I am using for the present fragment which include Marie Corelli, Swedenborg, St Thomas, the Sudanese war, Indian outcasts, Women under English Law, a description of St Helena, Flammarion's The End of the World, scores of children's singing games from Germany, France, England and Italy and so on. . . . '[6] Now, it's hard to see any reference to Swedenborg in the chapter, but we can turn to notebook VI.B.33 and on page 187 we will find the following item:

> new teeth grew
> at 81 in ES

Taking 81 as our clue, we can inspect Hart's *Concordance* to find whether the number appears in FW, and we will instantly locate the following phrase:

> got a daarlingt babyboy bucktooth, the thick of a gobstick, coming on ever so nerses nursely, gracies to goodess, at 81 (242.08-10)

We can now be very confident about the item we require as we look for the right biography. George Trobridge's *A Life of Emanuel Swedenborg* has it:

Cuno wrote. . . When I dined with him the last time at
Mr Odon's, he told me that a new set of teeth was growing in his mouth; and who has ever heard this of a man
eighty-one years old?[7]

Proceeding thence we can see more Swedenborg on
the same II.1 page. His involvement with geology
gives 'geolgian' in line six, and at the top of the page
'Mr Heer Assassor Neelson' refers to his being Assessor Extraordinary of the Royal College of Mines
from 1716 to 1747. But without the initial impetus
from the notebook, using this very obscure remark
about Swedenborg's teeth, we would be unlikely to
see him on the page at all. I had in fact assumed the
first line to be an allusion to Herr Assessor William
Afham, the assumed author of Part II of Kierkegaard's
Either/Or.

Many Buffalo notebooks include word-lists of
various kinds. For example, the Rhaeto-Romanic
words we used to gloss the account of the tailor's
daughter, or the Kiswahili words we mentioned in our
last chapter. It was on account of this that I was able
to claim that Joyce knew *siku* was Kiswahili for 'day'
when he inserted it into the text. Matthew Hodgart
pointed it out in his 'Word-Hoard', the first paper to be
printed by the *Newslitter* when it went into letterpress in 1964.[8] Hodgart transcribed the list, and also
those in Albanian and Basque, defining the words and
locating them in FW. He would have gone further had
not Dalton asked him to stop, insisting that he would
complete the task himself. But Dalton's work never
appeared and little was done with the notebooks during the 1960s. In 1968 Leo Knuth published studies

of the Dutch and Malay lists[9] and Hodgart used the Lithuanian list for a piece in *A Wake Digest*[10] Rather more was done during the 1970s.

To illustrate the principles I shall reproduce here a notebook list which was used exclusively in the Lord-Mayor's speech closing III.3 (FW 532-554). As the speech concentrates very heavily on Dublin trivia Joyce decorated it with extracts from the 'Dublin Annals' which occur at the end of *Thom's Dublin Directory*. Atherton[11] has already indicated some usage of this matter, but none of his examples derives from the list in VI.B.29, pages 156-7. Firstly, I shall transcribe the list, lettering the items in it from *a* to *v* and setting opposite them the appropriate entries from the *Annals*. When Joyce used a notebook item he would normally delete it in coloured crayon; deletion is indicated here by the use of an asterisk.

NOTEBOOK VI.B.29, 156	DUBLIN ANNALS
a Two toothed locust worms*	897. Ireland visited with a plague of strange worms, having two teeth, which devoured everything green in the land; supposed to have been locusts.
b our most noble*	962. About this time, Edgar, king of England, is said to have subdued part of Ireland, and particularly the most noble city of Dublin.
c ransom of beeves*	1029. Aulaffe Sitric, king of the

Danes of Dublin, taken prisoner by Matthew O'Regan, and ransomed, on payment of 200 beeves, 80 horses, 3 ounces of gold, and a sword called Charles's sword.

d Roderick*

1177 . . . Dublin invested by Roderic O'Connor, king of Ireland, whose army is surprised and routed by the garrison . . . . 1177 . . . Murtagh O'Connor, then at war with his father Roderic . . .

e Thomas Cusack

1409. Thomas Cusack chosen first mayor of Dublin. . .

f homage & felony*

1446. . . . Also John David, an armourer, having charged his master, William Catur, with treason, a combat took place, in which the latter, being intoxicated, was slain. David was hanged for felony shortly after.

1488. Sir Richard Edgecombe arrives in Dublin to take the homage and oaths of fealty of the great men of Ireland.

g Claret*

1490. The first importation of claret into Dublin.

h Browne embraces the Reformation*

1535. George Browne, archbishop of Dublin, embraces the Reformation.

i Last of the Bailiffs shall be the first of the sheriffs* 1548. The title of bailiffs of Dublin changed to that of sheriffs. . .

j Hawkins - spud* 1565. . . .John Hawkins, from Santa Fe, New Spain, introduced potatoes into Ireland.

NOTEBOOK
VI.B.29, 157.

k tenenure* Not in *Annals*.

l quo warranto* 1686. The city charter renewed by James II. under a quo warranto. . .

m packet placed 1696. A packet boat, with eighty passengers, lost at Sutton in Howth; the captain and a boy only saved.

n wooden shrouds 1733* 1733. The custom of burying in wooden shrouds introduced. . .

o circumference 7½* 1746. The circumference of Dublin ascertained to be seven miles and a quarter.

p Imperial Standard hoisted* 1801. Imperial Standard hoisted on Dublin Castle. . .

q All souls lost 1807. . . . The Prince of Wales Parkgate packet, and Rochdale transport, with 300 passengers, wrecked at Dunleary; all souls on board lost, except the captain and the crews.

r skin sick* 1817. . . .Infirmary for Diseases of the Skin opened.

s Asiatic cholera	1832. . . . Asiatic cholera raged virulently throughout Ireland for several months.
t Lanyon	Not in *Annals.*
u Benson	Not in *Annals.*
v Dargan	1852. June 24th. – £20,000 (subsequently increased by £6,000) placed at the disposal of the Royal Dublin Society by Wm. Dargan, esq., railway contractor, to be applied to an Exhibition of Irish Manufactures and other produce in Dublin, in 1853.

Thom's prepared their chronicle from earlier records, sometimes inaccurately. Warburton, Whitelaw and Walsh's *A History of the City of Dublin* (1818) gives the same entries for 1733 and 1746, but in the former case the shrouds are, more reasonably, woollen, and in the latter the city's circumference is 7¾ miles (note that Joyce's figure is different again).

As with many notebook lists the B.29 one follows the sequence of items in its source, simplifying our task in locating inconspicuous quotations. With *f* we have given the only uses of the words 'homage' and 'felony' between 1409 and 1490; with *m* the only use of 'packet' between 1686 and 1733 (there is no 'placed'). The more apocryphal annals, such as the appearance of two moons in 1339[12], were eventually dropped by Thom's, but in none of their directories was I able to locate the origins of *k*, *t* and *u*. Only the first of these, however, was used for FW: 'tenenure' is clearly a compound of 'tenure' with the Dublin district of Terenure.

Joyce produced his list, and also much of the speech for which it was used, in 1929. A typescript of the speech, now British Museum Add. MS 47484B. 426-460, was delivered in early 1930 to the publishers Babou and Kahane, who brought it out in June as a book entitled *Haveth Childers Everywhere.* If we examine the typescript, we find items clearly derived from the notebook list forming additions to it, either written in, or typed in a set of corrigenda at the end. Every entry Joyce deleted in crayon has been used, and also entry *e* which he presumably forgot to delete. There is more of a problem with *q*, which is already represented in the typed portion of the witness. Joyce may have forgotten when making the list that he had already used it.

Here is a dissected version of the relevant part of *Haveth Childers*, based on the typescript. All additions are italicized, and items deriving from the notebook are labelled with the appropriate letters.

Nova Tara, *our most noble* [b] . . .presently, *like Browne umbracing Christina Anya,*[h] after the Irishers. . . I will pay my pretty decent trade price for my glueglue gluecose, peebles, were it even as this is, the legal eric for infelicitous conduict (*here incloths placefined my pocket-anchoredcheck*)[m] and. . .I will put my oathhead unner my whitepot *for ransom of beeves* [c] and will stand me . . . by *Roderick's* [d] our most-monolith . . . I will say, hotelmen, that since I . . . not a bottlenim, *vanced* [changed from 'hoisted'] *imperial standard* [p] *by weaponright and* platzed mine residenze . . . here where *my tenenure* [k] *of office and* my toils of domestication first began . . .famine with Englisch sweat and oppedemics, *the twotoothed dragon worms* [a] *with allsort serpents* has compolitely seceded from this landleague of many nations. . . *The end of our aldest mosest ist the beginning of all thisorder so the last of their hansbailiffs* [changed from '*benbailiffs*'] *shall the first in our sheriffsby.* [i] New highs for all! . . . Seven ills *so* barely havd I habt, seaventy seavens *for circumference* [o] inkeptive are your hill prospect . . . Who can tell their tale whom I filled ad liptum on the plain of Soulsbury? With three hunkered peepers and twa and twas! [q] . . . tuberclerosies I reized *spudfully* from the *murphy*plantz [changed from '*Hawkins*plantz', itself changed from 'spudplantz'] *Hawkinsonia* [j] and berriberries . . . redmaids and ble*u*cotts [changed from 'bluecotts'], *in hommage all and felony,* [f] *fair home overcrowded* . . . *claret* [g] *cellar cobwebbed since the pontificate of Leo* . . . he is dummed (*clayed sheets, pineshrouded* [n] , *wake not, wolk not!*) [changed from 'Wake not! Walk not!'] *Quo warranto* [l] [changed from '*Wherefore*'] has his greats my . . . lord V. king regards for me . . . and to my saffronbreathing mongoloid, *the skinsyg* [r] , I gave Biorwiks powlver and uliv's oils . . . our lewd mayers and our lairdie meiresses . . . oilclothed over for cohabitation and allpointed by Hind: *Tamlane the*

Cussacke^{*e*} [changed from '*Cusacke*'] . . . [13]

This is an extraordinary way to produce a book. Of course the *Annals* are, in a sense, part of Dublin, but many of the quotations are so slender as to be quite invisible without the help of the notebook. For example 'our most noble' is quoted directly from Edgar's charter but Joyce's apparent intention was that it should be 'Edgar's charter *via* the Annals'. That presumably is the correct gloss. But 'Roderick' is spelled with a 'k' both in the notebook and FW. It would be downright perverse to connect him in glossary to a source which gives his name as 'Roderic'. And 'pocketanchoredcheck' is adequately defined as a pocket handkerchief plus a cheque anchored in m's pocket: it is most undesirable that we should have a packet boat anchored in the area too.

The same kinds of problem turn up with the many language lists in the notebooks. Matthew Hodgart finds the technique 'unjustifiable. . . He drew up lists of key words in several dozen languages, and at a very late stage in the revision of the text he threw them in, in a casual and even random manner, as if using a pepper-pot. Since he did not know these languages he often made mistakes, or so the experts tell us. The result is a wilful obscuring of that which was already highly obscure'.[14]

FW, as we have seen, is essentially a cycle. Like *Ulysses* it is an individual structure whose parts also possess an ordained individuality, partly in consequence of their style, partly in consequence of the clusters they contain. The nature of the clusters

appears to me suited to their contexts in most cases,
but to a degree this feeling may be simply the result
of repetitive reading. Why exactly did Joyce select
just these items from Thom's *Annals*? Diseases of the
skin could be fitted into the pattern, but not Asiatic
cholera. 'Homage' and 'felony' are commonplace
words; why did he not quote 1605 on the abolition
of tanistry and gavelkins?

When James Atherton says, in the context of
Bruno's 'coincidence of contraries', that 'Each word
tends to reflect in its own structure the structure of
the *Wake*'[15], he is not being at all theoretical. Some
words reflect the structure literally, usually at the
expense of meaningful content, approximating to
quadrifid onomatopoeia. Short phrases may telescope
the birth/thunder - marriage - death - resurrection pattern of its four Books. For instance 117.03-6:

> The lightning look, the birding cry, awe from the grave,
> everflowing on the times. Feueragusaria iordenwater;
> now godsun shine on menday's daughter; a good clap, a
> fore marriage, a bad wake, tell hell's well

which also includes the four elements. Ambivalence, as in some of the Book IV words in our first
chapter, may become a figure of the mirroring of
parts in the *Wake*. For example 'Downaboo' (054.01)
which means 'Up with Down' (Irish *An Dún abú* -
(County) Down to Victory!).[16] Or 'cald' (219.18),
which sounds like 'cold' but looks like Italian *caldo*,
meaning 'hot'. Or in personal names: 'Ouida Nooikke'
(221.28) is composed of French *oui* and Russian *da*
('yes') with no plus Danish *ikke* ('not').[17] Or 595.19:

'You are alpsulumply wroght', i.e. absolutely right or absolutely wrong, but nothing in between.

FW contains enough examples of this kind of thing for a sort of contagion to impart the same universality to all the other words. Significance, whatever it is, accumulates in FW like electrical energy. For Joyce to have been able to insert an element into the whole, it may have had to possess private significance for him at the outset, but once there its significance became the objective consequence of its position. A FW word is not, so far as I am concerned, the same thing as a word in the book you are now reading. It is a solid entity, a weird beautiful crystal, one of whose faces is perhaps identical with a fragment of *Thom's Dublin Directory*, but which in its totality is entirely subservient to the Wakean rules of play.

Nobody can predict just how much more explication of the *Wake* will blossom from the notebook studies, but I feel that once everything possible has been achieved, only a small proportion of the text will be accounted for. The notebooks are fine illustrations˙ of how much it is reasonable to expect of FW, and cannot be ignored, but we must not allow ourselves to become hypnotised by them. An unreasonable gloss—say one that depends on a statement that Joyce misread his own handwriting—ought not to be forced down the reader's throat. Most of the allusions in FW are reasonable.

When I read the notebooks in 1969-71 it was primarily the sigla which interested me, but I also copied everything I could recognize as occurring in FW. I collated my transcriptions with the insertions in the British Museum material, producing a list of witness numbers for each notebook. By selecting the earliest witness, and assuming it was not constructed too long after the notebook it drew on, I was able to build up a notebook chronology which was published in the *Newslitter* in 1972.[18] Some of my dating has been improved upon by the *Archive* editors (Hayman and Rose) and I expect to comment further upon the subject at some future point. But in 1972 I was tired of the notebooks and I postponed consideration of their sigla.

After the move to Scotland my interest in visiting other Joyceans also declined and my correspondence slid almost to a standstill. By a strange coincidence, the University of Dundee had an entomology unit and they were seeking a research assistant at just the time I arrived. I moved into a cottage in a tiny village a few miles outside the city and began work on *Annotations to FW.* Combining my notes with Hart's I produced a typescript of which copies were dispatched to Hodgart, Knuth and Senn. They eventually returned them to me, covered with additional data. Years later, Adaline Glasheen and Louis Mink would add more to the same sheets.

Dundee is a dull town but very conveniently centred as regards the then more stimulating locales of Stirling University, Edinburgh and pre-oil boom Aberdeen. More ambitious trips took me to such places as Iona and Orkney, where I wrote a chapter which was published in Begnal and Senn's *A Conceptual Guide to Finnegans Wake.*[19] Then in 1973 Hart left to take up the Professorship of Literature at

Essex University, where the *Newslitter* is now produced. My grant expired in the summer, and I was
becoming increasingly convinced that to achieve a
really total appreciation of the FW text I needed to
move permanently to Ireland. So again I loaded the
car with everything I owned, drove to Stranraer, and
took the car ferry, in a very similar frame of mind to
that in which I had arrived.

6
Ireland and
FINNEGANS WAKE

When I got to Ireland I found there wasn't much demand there for grasshopper acousticians. For a year I had a job as a quality control chemist with a pharmaceutical company who were extracting alkaloids from Irish ergot. Eventually I found the nine to five regime incompatible with my lifestyle and I became a part-time biology teacher. I also spent a couple of summers as curator of the James Joyce Tower in Sandycove, which was tolerable enough except for the tourists ('James Joyce? Who's he?').

The aesthetic assets of the country clearly outweigh the fiscal drawbacks, irrespective of Joycean connotations. As concerns the latter, most of the commentary that has appeared has examined Dublin in the context of *Ulysses*.[1] Clive Hart tells us[2] that 'The topography of Dublin is "on the page" at least as much as are the meanings of the words "priest", "kidney" or "ineluctable modality": it is a part of the book's primary reference system, without which its full sense cannot be apprehended. While nothing, or almost nothing, is incomprehensible without a knowledge of Dublin, everything, or almost everything, acquires a significant new dimension when local facts are explored.'

There is a good instance of such extradimensionality in Hart's essay on *The Wandering Rocks*. 'I undertook, on foot in Dublin, a literal form of 'practical criticism', timing the various routes taken by the characters, and also gathering information about the frequency of trams, the normal speed of a cavalcade, etc. . . . The results of the calculations based on these investigations are shown in the chart, which makes clear that 'Wandering Rocks' is constructed so as to be, in terms of timing, realistically exact'.[3]

To what extent is 'practical criticism' of value in FW studies? Louis Mink considers that 'The *Wake's* Dublin is very different from the real Dublin, but it is derived from it. Strictly speaking, it is largely derived from books *about* the real Dublin, since so many of its allusions are to a past Dublin reconstructed only in its histories.'[4] As these books can be obtained anywhere—witness Mink's use of interlibrary loans to conduct prodigious investigations of medieval Dublin from Connecticut—one might argue that FW can be researched with equal ease anywhere. But in practice easy access counts for a lot, and in the National Library there is a truly elephantine volume of printed matter relating to the country and its capital. There are also many Irish songs in FW, and simple cognizance of the words quoted is a poor substitute for having heard the original. In spite of recordings, many of these songs are extremely hard to come by abroad.

What Hart is talking about, however, is largely the result of walking the Dublin streets and noticing what is there. We might look at a specimen of FW from this

platform and see if it improves it. The passage taken
from Edgar Quinet's account of Vico (281.04-13),
which is repeatedly parodied through the book,[5]
achieves one of its most lyrical transformations in the
immemorial dance of II.1:

> Since the days of Roamaloose and Rehmoose the
> pavanos have been strident through their struts of
> Chapelldiseut, the vaulsies have meed and youdled
> through the purly ooze of Ballybough, many a mismy
> cloudy has tripped taintily along that hercourt strayed
> reelway and the rigadoons have held ragtimed revels on
> the platauplain of Grangegorman (236.19-24)

A simple version of the first-level narrative would
run as follows: Since the days of Romulus and Remus
(German *Reh*, deer, relates to 'moose'[6]), people
dancing the pavan ('the proud pavan'[7]) have been
striding and strutting through the streets of Chapelizod. Others, dancing the waltz, have met and
yodelled—and said 'me' and 'you' to one another—
through the purlieus of Ballybough. Miss McCloud's
Reel (which is played near the end of 'Clay' in
Dubliners) has been tripped daintily along Harcourt
Street Railway, and lively rigadoons have been
danced at Grangegorman.

To what extent is direct experience of Chapelizod,
Ballybough, Harcourt Street and Grangegorman of
assistance in understanding this? We'll begin with the
second two localities.

Harcourt Street Railway Station has been disused
for some years, but the building is still visible. Its
tracks, leading away to the South, have been effect-
ively obliterated in the inner city. Grangegorman, on

the opposite side of Dublin, also contains a disused station, the Broadstone Terminus, with the remains of its tracks running away to the North. If one stands on Constitution Hill and looks up at the Broadstone it does indeed appear to rest on a sort of plateau, which extends in the direction of the Richmond Lunatic Asylum. Joyce may have felt that ragtime and lunacy belonged together, but the main point of the selection was the representation of North and South by the diametrically opposed termini.

Although Ballybough is further North than Grangegorman, it is also much further to the East, just as Chapelizod is much further to the West. Microcosmic sequences of cardinal points are another instance of the words of FW reflecting its structure, the four sides of ◻ , and are abundant. In this instance it will be observed that the standard progression, North-South - East - West, has been reversed.

Every FW reader knows that Chapelizod was Isolde's chapel, *Chapelle d'Iseut,* but a concrete image enhances the impact by emphasizing how few streets of any description it contains. Only the central region between Chapelizod Bridge and Le Fanu's 'House by the Churchyard' can be suggested: this is so small that anything strident in one part of it would be audible throughout the rest.

For Joyce, Ballybough is an odoriferous environment. See 095.02-3: 'Do I mind? I mind the gush off the mon like Ballybock manure works on a tradewinds day.' As Mink says, 'Vitriol works at Ballybough Bridge were operated by the Dublin and Wicklow Manure Co, Ltd.'[8] The present river Tolka, however, contains less 'purly ooze' than in the days of Mud Island. In *Portrait*, V, Stephen crosses the bridge on his walk from 8 Royal Terrace, Fairview, to Stephen's Green: 'he foreknew that as he passed the sloblands of Fairview he would think of the cloistral silverveined prose of Newman'. The district also features in the Lord-Mayor's speech: 'I let faireviews in on slobodens but ranked rothgardes round wrathmindsers' (541.25-6). Here we have another contrast of North and South Dublin. In the North, the Lord-Mayor considers that he has opened attractive prospects on to the sloblands. In the South, he has stationed gardai (police) in comparatively peaceful Rathgar, which encloses the Southern perimeter of less peaceful Rathmines. To fully appreciate the antinomy between the two sides of the city, it is necessary to listen to people from each half deriding the other half. Mink gives a number of instances of North/South pairings.[9]

It has been said that the Hill of Howth and the Rock of Gibraltar merge at the end of *Ulysses*. The personification of the hill as m has a precedent in 'Nausicaa':

> Howth settled for slumber tired of long days, of yumyum rhododendrons (he was old) and felt gladly the night breeze lift, ruffle his fell of ferns. He lay but opened a red eye unsleeping, deep and slowly breathing, slumberous but awake.[10]

In contrast, Joyce's brightest evocation of the hill is the one at the close of FW. It is a child's-eye view from the city, looking East across Dublin Bay. The rising sun animates the cumulus clouds over Howth, evoking aspirations of paradisiac celluloid escape:

> We might call on the Old Lord, what do you say? There's something tells me. He is a fine sport. Like the score and a moighty went before him. And a proper old promnentory. . . . He might knight you an Armor elsor daub you the first cheap magyerstrape. Remember Bomthomanew vim vam vom Hungerig. Hoteform, chain and epolettes, botherbumbose. And I'll be your aural eyeness. But we vain. Plain fancies. It's in the castles air. My currant bread's full of sillymottocraft. (623.04-19)

The trams, alas, have gone, although the National Library preserves their timetables. The Sutton and Howth Electric Tramway ran to the Summit of Howth but 081.16-18 has it stop at Clontarf: 'not where his dreams top their traums halt (Beneathere! Benathere!) but where livland yontide meared with the wilde, saltlea with flood'. The tram conductor is shouting the Irish name of Howth, *Beinn Éadair.*[11] On the preceding page another conductor, on a Westbound tram, asks if there are any passengers continuing past Chapelizod to Lucan: 'Issy-la-Chapelle! Any lucans, please?' (080.36)

It is possible to resolve Dublin in FW into a mesh of emotions: rivalry between the North and South sides, and nostalgic yearning towards Howth in the East and various points on the Liffey in the West, notably Chapelizod, Lucan and Leixlip. The detailed account of Chapelizod in 264.21-265.28[12], 'By this riverside, on our sunnybank, how buona the vista, by Santa Rosa! . . . ', includes several houses whose names are still there to see, for instance Sunnybank,

Buena Vista and Santa Rosa. But the majority have gone: Joycean Dublin is fast vanishing.

Leixlip, meaning 'Salmon Leap', is represented as the homing point towards which the four-year-old salmon attempts to return, to spawn. 280.06-8: 'tomorrows gone and yesters outcome as Satadays afternoon lex leap smiles on the twelvemonthsminding'. 460.28-30: 'Splesh of hiss splash springs your salmon. Twick twick, twinkle twings my twilight as Sarterday afternoon lex leap will smile on my fourinhanced twelvemonthsmind.' The actual Salmon Leap at Leixlip has been destroyed by the hydroelectric scheme now operating there.

This Western inclination, most prominent in I.8, is ultimately directed towards the source of the Liffey in the Wicklow Mountains: the river sweeps round in an arc so its source is actually South, not West, of the city, but we are just looking in the direction from which the water arrives. The mountains, of course, are amongst the finest scenery in the country, and one of the great advantages in living in Dublin is the facility with which one can move from shops and crowded streets to rocks and heather with no human artifact in sight.

A new problem emerges here. When we are inspired by the scenery, let us say, of Glendalough, in the mountains, and we consider the important role played by it in Book IV, we must not be led to deduce that a recollection of that scenery inspired Joyce to write the passage. Joyce, for all we know, may never have been at Glendalough. He places St Kevin on an island: there are no islands on either lake, and such is the volume of literature dealing with the site that it is unthinkable that this could be the result of an error. Splendid as it is in the light of early morning, Glendalough is for Joyce a far less realistic proposition than Howth.

It can, in fact, be claimed that realism in FW declines logarithmically with distance from the city centre. It can be claimed that much of FW views Ireland through the consciousness of the Dubliner who has travelled little and does not think of Irish placenames in particularly spatial terms. There is a sad tendency amongst many Dubliners to look down on the inhabitants of the countryside, but of course Irish placenames will be more familiar than foreign ones. Mink feels that topographical 'conflations sound like the amusing misperception of names by an ear attuned only to hearing Irish ones: Bulgaria is heard as Ballygarry, an otherwise not very important village, and the Balearic Islands as the Ballyhoura mountains.'[13]

The correct interpretation of this effect, as I see it, is that Dublin reality gives expression to one particularly sharp and unequivocal layer of FW narrative. Take the three visions shown to Yawn on 486.14-33. At the first his inquisitor exclaims 'Pious, a pious person.', at the second 'Purely, in a pure manner.' and at the third 'Bellax, acting like a bellax.' This is usually glossed with Vico's epithet of religious wars, '*Pia e pura bella*'[14], but the Dubliner will identify the last immediately as 'Bollocks, acting like a bollocks.' One consequence of the technique is to set the Dubliner at a perpetual advantage in discussions on the meaning of FW.

This is not to say that the only distinction between the parts of Ireland in FW is that of 'real' Dublin as against the 'unreal' countryside. The four old men who are questioning Yawn, for example, are figures of the four provinces of Ireland. 'Bellax, acting like a bellax' is said by Luke Tarpey, as representing Dublin (in Leinster). Mark Lyons, who stands for Cork (in Munster) speaks like this:

> Dorhqk. And sure where can you have such good old chimes anywhere, and *leave* you, as on the Mash and how'tis I would be engaging you with my plovery soft accents and descanting upover the scene beunder me of your loose vines in their hairafall with them two loving loofs braceleting the slims of your ankles and your mouth's flower rose and sinking ofter the soapstone of silvry speech. (140.21-7)

The Belfast and Galway voices are likewise caricatures, as though like topography, character has been filtered through a membrane which recognizes Dublin alone as valid. This cannot be accounted for simply by saying that Joyce had seen little of the Irish countryside. We know, for instance, that he visited the Aran Islands, for he published an account of them in a Trieste newspaper in 1912. 'The Mirage of the Fisherman of Aran' describes its subject: 'He dresses in wool as thick as felt and wears a big black hat with a wide brim.'[15] He is reduced in FW 121.11-14 to a detail in an illuminated manuscript, '*the Aranman ingperwhis* [whispering] *through the hole of his hat*'. A good deal of this paragraph is based on Sir Edward Sullivan's introduction to *The Book of Kells,* so the Aranman has been safely encapsulated in an exhibit at Trinity College Library, Dublin.

It might follow from all this that a group of Dubliners examining, say, the portion of FW that the European FW Study Group examined, might uncover some very germinal facts. A FW study group was in fact set up by the James Joyce Institute of Ireland in 1975, dealing with various parts of that chapter (II.3). The problems of housing and catering for participants did not arise: people simply arrived at Newman House every Tuesday evening and worked through a page of 'Butt and Taff' or 'The Norwegian Captain'. Unfortunately, few of them appreciated the basic axioms of the *Wake*, and I eventually tired of having to apologise for Rhaeto-Romanic and the like. I was also somewhat exasperated by the modesty of the people in respect of their own guesses, which could prevent valuable overtones from being voiced.

At odd times a really useful interpretation would surface. For instance, everyone in the European group knew that 'the Riss, the Ross, the sur of all Russers' (340.35) was not only the Czar of all the Russias but also the St Stephen's Day chant 'The Wren, the Wren, the King of all Birds'. Hodgart and Worthington quote the line.[16] But a Mr Brady in the Dublin group was able to add that the sentence four lines above, 'Hyededye, kittyls, and howdeddoh, pan!' comes from the same source. 'Up with the kettle and down with the pan, And give us a penny to bury the Wren' [pronounced 'rann'].

Despite the timid advances of the study group, there is no doubt that the language, mythology and folklore of Ireland are so much a part of FW that at times book and country seem almost complementary halves of a pattern. There is in present-day Ireland a desperate need to justify insistence on local culture in the face of cosmopolitan survival. Does not FW, with its earthshaking reputation, constitute a valuable spearhead of such culture? Does not the blending in it of numerous foreign tongues assist its penetration where such tongues are spoken? Is it not curious that the Irish fail to exploit this gift?

Joyce is slowly becoming respectable in Ireland. In consequence of the extremely bad image he was given by the popular press in the 1920s many of the older generation still see him as noxious. I have the impression that there are people who regard *Ulysses* as an analogue of those medieval grimoires, merely to open which conferred instantaneous damnation. Until the end of the 1950s no Irish bookseller would touch the book, although Hodges Figgis Ltd were prepared to write to its publisher and arrange to have it sent to you directly. There is a common notion that it is something to do with drinking, a kind of verbalized vomit. Following the lead of Flann O'Brien, there is a strong tendency, especially in public houses, to distort all facts pertaining to Joyce, to ascribe to him opinions and statements he never uttered.

Amongst the greatest stumbling blocks is the failure to comprehend that famous aesthetic theory in the *Portrait*. 'The personality of the artist, at first a cry or a cadence or a mood and then a fluid and lambent narrative finally refines itself out of existence, impersonalizes itself, so to speak.' The elderly beer-swilling Dubliner sees in *Ulysses* merely the handing out of what he regards as Joyce's personal opinions, expressions of anti-Irish rancour and disgust. This interpretation can be sustained only by keeping one's experience of the book at a bare minimum, and rejecting all critical commentaries as the fantasies of deluded aliens.

As more people read *Ulysses* with greater care, and preferably with reference to the saner commentaries such as Thornton, Gilbert and Budgen, the voices of the bigots will cease. A similar change of aesthetic attitudes might be observed, say, with the Burren of Clare. Nineteenth-century guidebooks to Ireland tend to glorify such localities as Killarney, but the Burren is dismissed as a dreary mass of infertile stone. Modern guidebooks eulogize its landscape as amongst the most enthralling in the country. In the same way we will eventually see *Ulysses* and FW accepted as natural Irish phenomena, albeit a little harsh on the body.

The need of the FW exegete to experience Dublin and Ireland is attested by the number of authorities I have met passing through the city, during my residence there. Ignoring the period of the Joyce Symposium in June 1977, I have met Jack Dalton, Adaline Glasheen, Clive Hart, Louis Mink, Brendan O Hehir, Fritz Senn and Mabel Worthington, to consider only names appearing elsewhere in this volume. Danis Rose and Petr Skrabanek actually live in Dublin. Skrabanek, a Czech neurologist, is particularly noteworthy for his list of Slavonic words in FW[17], and also for having produced the only extant study of Anglo-Irish words in FW.[18]

More Wakean scholarship will appear as we move into the 1980s. At Berkeley Brendan O Hehir is producing *A Finnegans Wake Polyglossary*, a very large compendium of foreign language glosses. Rose's synoptic version is presumably to be expected at length, and it is to be hoped that more Buffalo notebooks will be transcribed by someone. The centenary of Joyce's birth, in 1982, may provide an excuse for some kind of constructive upheaval. Eventually, when I feel like it, I'll produce new editions of *Sigla* and *Annotations*, but for the moment my attention has reverted to Myxomycetes, the Irish population being very poorly documented. I have resumed communication with the two major English experts on the group, Bruce Ing and David Mitchell. The acellular slime fungi of such places as Cork and Donegal are crying out for attention. The longer you neglect Joyce's works, the more satisfying they eventually become to return to. So for the present I'm giving *Finnegans Wake* a rest.

Notes

CHAPTER 1

1. Brendan O Hehir and John Dillon: *A Classical Lexicon for Finnegans Wake*. Berkeley, Los Angeles and London: University of California Press, 1977, 130.
2. Petr Skrabanek: 'Structure and Motif in Thunderwords: A Proposal'. *AWN* (*A Wake Newslitter*) XII.6, 1975, 109.
3. Samuel Beckett: 'Dante . . . Bruno. Vico . . Joyce', in *Our Exagmination round his Factification for Incamination of Work in Progress*. London: Faber and Faber, 1929, 5.
4. Helmut Bonheim: *A Lexicon of the German in Finnegans Wake*. Berkeley, Los Angeles and London: University of California Press, 1967, 55.
5. Louis O. Mink: *A Finnegans Wake Gazetteer*. Bloomington and London: Indiana University Press, 1978, 48.
6. James Joyce: *Ulysses* (1922). London: The Bodley Head, 1960, 15.
7. Richard Ellmann: *James Joyce* (1959). Oxford University Press, 1966, 565.
8. The first Rhaeto-Romanic List appeared under 'Margadant' in the Appendix to James S. Atherton's *The Books at the Wake*, London: Faber and Faber, 1959, 266 (Second edition, Mamaroneck, New York: Paul P. Appel, 1974, 271). An expanded version by Fritz Senn, 'rheadoromanscing', was given in *AWN*, old series, 11, 1963, 1-2. Danis Rose has annotated the Rhaeto-Romanic list from Buffalo Notebook VI.B.46: see his *James Joyce's The Index Manuscript: Fin-*

negans Wake Holograph Workbook VI.B.46. Colchester: A Wake Newslitter Press, 1978, 8-13.

9.   Bjorn J. Tysdahl: *Joyce and Ibsen.* Oslo: Norwegian Universities Press, 1968, appendix.

10.   Matthew J.C. Hodgart and Mabel P. Worthington: *Song in the Works of James Joyce.* New York: Columbia University Press, 1959, 129.

11.   See under 'Stella and Vanessa' in Adaline Glasheen: *A Third Census of Finnegans Wake.* Berkeley, Los Angeles and London: University of California Press, 1977, 271.

12.   Bonheim, *Lexicon of the German,* 102.

13.   Brendan O Hehir: *A Gaelic Lexicon for Finnegans Wake.* Berkeley, Los Angeles and London: University of California Press, 1967, 171.

14.   Bonheim: *Lexicon of the German,* 136.

15.   O Hehir and Dillon: *Classical Lexicon,* 406.

16.   P.W. Joyce: *Irish Names of Places* (First Series). Yorkshire: EP Publishing, 1972, 160-1.

17.   Mink: *Gazetteer,* 462.

18.   Mink: *Gazetteer,* 502.

19.   Stuart Gilbert (ed.) *Letters of James Joyce* I. London: Faber and Faber, 1957, 214: 'Shawn . . . is written in the form of a *via crucis* of 14 stations' (Joyce to Miss Weaver, 24 May 1924). One attempt to locate the stations was made by Ian MacArthur (Structure and Motif in Jaun'), *AWN* XV.5, 1978, 67-73.

20.   Glasheen: *Third Census,* 183.

21.   Luigi Schenoni: Italian List for III.3 to appear in *AWN.*

22.   Bonheim: *Lexicon of the German,* 137: '*Klee:* clover'.

23.   A.M.L. Knuth: *The Wink of the Word: A Study of James Joyce's Phatic Communication.* Amsterdam: Rodopi, 1976, 172.

24.   Bonheim: *Lexicon of the German,* 170.

25.   Luigi Schenoni: Italian List for IV to appear in *AWN.*

26.   B.P. Misra: 'Sanskrit Translations'. *AWN* I.6, 1964, 9. Professor E.G. Quin of Trinity College, Dublin, points out that Sanskrit *sārva-jīvana* means 'bringing everything to life'.

CHAPTER 2

1. *Ulysses,* 61.
2. *Ulysses,* 235.
3. *Ulysses,* 61-2.
4. *Ulysses,* 86-94.
5. Ellsworth Mason and Richard Ellmann (eds): *The Critical Writings of James Joyce.* New York: The Viking Press, 1959, 134n.
6. Glasheen: *Third Census,* 20. D.B. Christiani: *Scandinavian Elements of Finnegans Wake.* Evanston: Northwestern University Press, 1965, 117.
7. *Ulysses,* 59.
8. Rose: *The Index Manuscript,* 232-3.
9. O Hehir and Dillon: *Classical Lexicon,* 79-80.
10. Atherton: *Books,* 110-13.
11. Thomas Tompion, watchmaker, invented the dead-beat escapement (Glasheen: *Third Census* 287).
12. Gilbert: *Letters* I, 257-8.
13. Adaline Glasheen: 'Rough Notes on Joyce and Wyndham Lewis'. *AWN* VIII.5, 1971, 67-75.
14. Ellmann: *James Joyce,* 22, 411.
15. I was unaware at the time that Joyce's use of Frazer had already been examined by Nathan Halper, a New York art dealer, in an early paper, 'James Joyce and the Russian General', *Partisan Review,* XVIII, 1951, and I failed to acknowledge him in my study of the structure of FW written in 1968.
16. Atherton: *Books,* 157-61.

CHAPTER 3

1. Anthony Farrow: Review of Books on Joyce. *Cithara* XVII.1, 1977, 75.
2. Robert Martin Adams: *Surface and Symbol: The Consistency of James Joyce's Ulysses.* Oxford University Press, 1962, 86-7.

3. Weldon Thornton: *Allusions in Ulysses*. Chapel Hill: University of North Carolina Press, 1968.

4. Roland McHugh: *Annotations to Finnegans Wake*. Baltimore: Johns Hopkins University Press; London: Routledge and Kegan Paul, 1980.

5. Gilbert: *Letters* I, 247.

6. (Chapter I, note 3).

7. Stuart Gilbert: 'Prolegomena to Work in Progress', in *Our Exagmination*, 70.

8. T.E. Connolly (ed.): *James Joyce's Scribbledehobble: the Ur-Workbook for Finnegans Wake*. Evanston: Northwestern University Press, 1961, 142.

9. Joseph Campbell and Henry Morton Robinson: *A Skeleton Key to Finnegans Wake*. (New York: Harcourt, Brace, 1944). London: Faber and Faber, 1947, 16.

10. Campbell and Robinson: *Skeleton Key*, 265.

11. Adaline Glasheen: *A Census of Finnegans Wake*. London: Faber and Faber, 1956; *A Second Census of Finnegans Wake*. Evanston: Northwestern University Press, 1963; (*Third Census*, see chapter 1, note 11). (Other books: see chapter 1, notes 8 and 10).

12. Glasheen: *Census*, x-xi (Omitted from *Third Census*).

13. Atherton: *Books*, 23, 126.

14. Clive Hart and Fritz Senn (eds.): *A Wake Digest*. Sydney University Press, 1968; ix.

15. 'Opening Litter', *AWN* (old series) 1, 1962, 2.

16. Editorial, *AWN* (old series), 8, 1962, 2.

17. Clive Hart: *Structure and Motif in Finnegans Wake*. London: Faber and Faber, 1962, 17.

18. Hart: *Structure and Motif*, 16-18.

19. Hart: *Structure and Motif*, 67.

20. Roland McHugh: *The Sigla of Finnegans Wake*. London: Edward Arnold, 1976. Austin: University of Texas Press, 1977.

21. Clive Hart: *A Concordance to Finnegans Wake*. Minneapolis: University of Minnesota Press, 1963, 460-516.

22. (Chapter 2, note 6; chapter 1, notes 4 and 13).

23. In deference it must be added that the *Quarterly* has improved a little in more recent years, with some useful recol-

lections of Joyce by his contemporaries and occasional studies
of the *Ulysses* manuscripts. Alan Cohn's *James Joyce Checklist*
is a useful source of bibliographical data. But most issues still
contain a great deal of unconvincing academic bilge.

24. 'EXPLICATIONS – for the greeter glossary of code –
"Butt and Taff"'. *AWN* (old series), 5, 1962, 7-8.

25. The Armenian list in Notebook VI.B.46 is transcribed and
annotated in Rose's *Index Manuscript*. 'Siranouche' and
'Satenik' are explained there as women's names, (193).

26. Roland McHugh: 'A European *Finnegans Wake* Study
Group', in *Atti del Third International James Joyce Symposium*. University of Trieste, 1974, 313, 317-9.

CHAPTER 4

1. Clive Hart: 'Notes on the Text of *Finnegans Wake*'.
Journal of English and Germanic Philology, LIX, 1960, 229-39.

2. Philipp Wolff: 'Kiswahili Words in FW'. *AWN* (old series)
8, 1962, 2-4.

3. Jack P. Dalton: 'Re 'Kiswahili Words in FW' by Philipp
Wolff'. *AWN* (old series) 12, 1963, 6-10.

4. Michael Groden (general ed.): *The James Joyce Archive*.
New York: Garland Publications, 1977-8. Volumes 44-63:
'*Finnegans Wake:* Drafts, Typescripts and Proofs', edited by
David Hayman and Danis Rose.

5. Clive Hart: 'The Elephant in the Belly: Exegesis of *Finnegans Wake*'. *AWN* (old series) 13, 1963, 5. Reprinted with
modifications in Hart and Senn: *Wake Digest*, 7.

6. Hart and Senn: *Wake Digest*, 7.

7. (Chapter 3, note 5)

8. Hart: *Structure and Motif*, 29.

9. David Hayman: *A First-Draft Version of Finnegans Wake*.
Austin: University of Texas Press; London: Faber and Faber,
1963.

10. Jack P. Dalton: 'I Say It's Spinach - "Watch!" '. *AWN* (old
series) 17, 1963, 11.

11. Jack P. Dalton: 'Advertisement for the Restoration'. In

Jack P. Dalton and Clive Hart (eds.): *Twelve and a Tilly: Essays on the Occasion of the 25th Anniversary of Finnegans Wake*. Evanston: Northwestern University Press; London: Faber and Faber, 1965, 122.

12. Hugh Kenner: *The Computerized Ulysses. Harper's*, April 1980, 89-95.

13. Dalton and Hart: *Twelve and a Tilly*, 130.

14. Hart: 'Notes on the Text', 235.

15. Atherton: *Books*, 66.

16. *Our Exagmination*, 14.

17. Peter du Sautoy: 'The Published Text'. *AWN* IV.5, 1967, 98.

18. Ian MacArthur: *AWN* XIII.5, 1976, 91.

19. MacArthur: 'A Textual Study of III.4', *AWN* XIII.1, 1976, 3-8; 'A Textual Study of III.3', *AWN* XIII.3, 1976, 43-8, *AWN* XIII.5, 1976, 85-92; 'Butt and Taff - A Textual Study', *AWN* XIV. 1, 1977, 5-8.

20. MacArthur: 'The F Sigla'. *AWN* XV.4, 1978, 58.

CHAPTER 5

1.   Peter Spielberg: *James Joyce's Manuscripts and Letters at the University of Buffalo: A Catalogue*. University of Buffalo, 1962.

2.   Dalton and Hart: *Twelve and a Tilly*, 136.

3.   (Chapter 3, note 8).

4.   David Hayman: 'A List of Corrections for the Scribble-dehobble'. *James Joyce Quarterly*, I.2, 1964, 23-9.

5.   (Chapter 1, note 8).

6.   Gilbert: *Letters* I, 302.

7.   George Trobridge: *A Life of Emanuel Swedenborg*. London: Frederick Warne, 1912, 300.

8.   Matthew J.C. Hodgart: 'Word-Hoard'. *AWN* I.1, 1964, 1-5.

9.   Leo Knuth: 'Dutch Elements in FW pp.75-78 compared with Holograph Workook VI.B.46', *AWN* V.2, 1968, 19-28; 'Some Notes on Malay Elements in FW', *AWN* V.4, 1968, 51-63.

10. Matthew J.C. Hodgart: 'Some Lithuanian Words in FW' in Hart and Senn: *Wake Digest,* 59-61.

11. Atherton: *Books,* 92-3.

12. FW 502.11-14.

13. FW 535.08-550.30.

14. Matthew J.C. Hodgart: *James Joyce: A Student's Guide.* London: Routledge and Kegan Paul, 1978, 136.

15. Atherton: *Books,* 53.

16. O Hehir: *Gaelic Lexicon,* 36.

17. Christiani: *Scandinavian Elements,* 135.

18. Roland McHugh: 'Chronology of the Buffalo Notebooks'. *AWN* IX.2, 1972, 19-31; IX.3, 1972, 36-8; IX.5, 1972, 100.

19. Roland McHugh: 'Recipis for the Price of the Coffin', in Michael H. Begnal and Fritz Senn (eds.): *A Conceptual Guide to Finnegans Wake.* University Park and London: Pennsylvania University Press, 1974, 18-32.

CHAPTER 6

1. See for instance Adams: *Surface and Symbol* (c.f. chapter 3, note 2); J.C.C. Mays: 'Some Comments on the Dublin of *Ulysses',* in L. Bonnerot (ed.): *'Ulysses' cinquante ans après,* Paris: Didier, 1974, 83-98.

2. Clive Hart and Leo Knuth: *A Topographical Guide to James Joyce's Ulysses.* Colchester: A Wake Newslitter Press, 2nd ed., 1976, 18.

3. Clive Hart: 'Wandering Rocks', in Clive Hart and David Hayman (eds.): *James Joyce's Ulysses: Critical Essays.* Berkeley, Los Angeles and London: University of California Press, 1974, 200.

4. Mink: *Gazetteer,* xi.

5. Hart: *Structure and Motif,* 182-200.

6. Bonheim: *Lexicon of the German,* 74.

7. James Joyce: *Giacomo Joyce.* London: Faber and Faber, 1968, 9.

8. Mink: *Gazetteer,* 221.

9. Mink: *Gazetteer,* xxii-xxiii.

10. *Ulysses,* 494-5.

11. O Hehir: *Gaelic Lexicon*, 53.

12. Fritz Senn: 'The Localisation of Legend'. *AWN* VIII.1, 1971, 10-13.

13. Mink: *Gazetteer*, xx.

14. Hart: *Structure and Motif*, 238.

15. Mason and Ellmann: *Critical Writings*, 236.

16. Hodgart and Worthington: *Song*, 133.

17. Petr Skrabanek: '355.11 Slavansky Slavar, R. Slavyanskii Slovar (Slavonic Dictionary)' *AWN* IX.4, 1972, 51-68.

18. Petr Skrabanek: 'Anglo-Irish in FW'. *AWN* XIII.5, 1976, 79-85.

Index